Contents

Realis Estates Limited

Tomkinson Teal
Chartered Accountants

Foreword by
BRIAN LITTLE
Former Aston Villa manager 1994–1998

I BECAME THE manager of Aston Villa in November 1994. It was a club that I held very dear to my heart, as my entire playing career had been in the famous claret and blue. My first match in charge was a home game against Sheffield Wednesday on 27 November 1994, and it was a game that we drew 1-1. It was a spirited performance that pleased me but still kept us in the bottom three of the Premier League, so there could absolutely be no resting on laurels for me or the team.

My next game was a League Cup game away at Crystal Palace. Villa were the holders of the competition, but we fell 4-1. In both of the games, I had not picked Shaun Teale. Shaun had not played much under the previous regime and had picked up a few knocks in training, so he wasn't really in my thoughts in those early days.

I had been a striker in my playing days, but I always took the philosophy that to build a good team, a manager needs to look at his defence in the first instance. We had the likes of Dalian Atkinson, Dwight Yorke and Dean Saunders up front, so scoring goals was not really an issue. My next league game was away at my former club, Leicester City. I knew it was going to be a difficult return to Filbert Street on a number of levels, so I had to get the formation right. I decided that I would make some changes, so I brought in Shaun to take the left-hand side position in central defence. I had seen Shaun play with Paul McGrath in previous seasons and they had formed a very formidable partnership. I was interested to see how he would perform after being out for some time. We drew the game 1-1 with a good team performance. In particular, I noted Shaun's contributions.

He was very vocal and arranged the defence well. He gave me 100% and from then on, I picked him for the remainder of the season.

I won the Manager of the Month award in January 1995, and I honestly put it down to the contributions made by my defence, and Shaun was pivotal to its success, not only on the pitch but also off it, in places such as the training ground and the dressing room. Shaun had come from non-league football, and you always got the impression that he never took playing in the top division for granted.

We managed to stay up on the final day of the season; we drew with Norwich City at Carrow Road, and that point was enough, as Newcastle United beat our relegation rivals Crystal Palace. My mission to keep the club that I loved in top-flight football had been accomplished, and I was so proud of the players' contributions. They had bought into the philosophy that me, Allan Evans and John Gregory (my assistants) shared, and no one more so than Shaun Teale. He would take on our thoughts – and he wasn't afraid to give his opinions either. As a football manager, you get to experience the whole range of types of people you have at your disposal. The best ones are those you can trust to do the job on and off the pitch, and I can honestly say that Shaun fits perfectly into that category – he was a pleasure to manage.

When I was planning for the 1995–1996 season, I knew that Shaun was soon going to be out of contract. I was happy to offer him a new deal for another 12 months, and I told him and his agent of my intention. In the meantime, I had been approached by Tranmere Rovers, who could offer Shaun a longer and more lucrative contract. I was obliged to tell him, and he decided that this would be a better option for him and his wife, Carol, and their boys to move closer to the family back in the northwest.

Although for many years I thought Shaun wasn't too happy with me for this, now when we see each other, we have a good laugh about it.

Shaun is a person in the mould of how he played the game, always giving 100% honestly and openly. What you see is what you get with him. I always enjoy seeing him in our roles at Villa Park today, and we always have a lovely catch-up. He has a wonderful rapport with everyone at Aston Villa, staff and supporters alike. When Rob Carless, the ghost writer, asked me if I would like to say a few words in the foreword of this book, I said "yes" straight away.

It's been a pleasure – just like it was when Shaun played for me all those years ago.

Here's to you, Mr Teale!

CHAPTER ONE
1994
Celebrate the bullet

Saturday 29 January 1994
Blundell Park
Grimsby Town FC

I'M IN GRIMSBY and I am playing for my current team – Aston Villa. It's the FA Cup fourth round. It's wintertime, but today is quite mild and the pitch is not as cut up as it could have been. Fair play to the ground staff. Town are punching above their weight and play in the First Division, just one division below us. We are favourites to win this match. After all, we finished runners-up to Manchester United in the Premier League last season. We lost it by 10 points in the end, but we were never 10 points worse than them. We lost our last three games and United won theirs. Shit happens and it's life, but up to that point, it was neck and neck.

Anyway, that was last season.

We are under the cosh a little bit this season, as we have fallen down the league and are currently in tenth place. But we are going well in the Coca-Cola Cup, and in a few weeks' time, we play Tranmere Rovers away in the first leg of the semi-final, a chance to get to Wembley and win some silverware. Today is all about the FA Cup, though, and a good run in this competition will go some way towards banishing last season's disappointments. It's not going to be easy, but we can see the twin towers of Wembley stadium on the horizon. There are more than 15,000 fans in the stadium, and the vast majority are baying for our blood. Elsewhere the 'hacks' are waiting to write one of the headlines that typifies the old 'giant killing', but we are not in the mood to give them one!

We took the lead through Ray Houghton after some good work down the left by Dalian Atkinson. It's the 13th minute of the match and our nerves have settled. Ten minutes later and mine are well and truly frayed, as I'm sent off alongside Grimsby's Steve Livingstone. We both went up for a long ball played up by their keeper. Livingstone caught me on the bridge of my nose and it fucking stings. We both go to the ground and tussle with each other for a few seconds before every man and his dog gets involved. It was over in seconds in reality, and my top is torn, baring my chest, and weirdly, my shoulder blades are also on display. I look like Lou Ferrigno from that TV programme *The Incredible Hulk* – minus the muscles and with a moustache!

The referee calls us both over. We have made peace with each other, but the man in black decides to turn the match into his show and gives us both the red card. The reason – because we were fighting! Er, no, we hadn't been. It was handbags at dawn and a falling over with a few pushes. The game was shown on *Match of the Day* as one of the main matches and even the commentator, Tony Gubba, couldn't quite get it. Apparently, the ref had 'followed the letter of the law'. One thing that everyone on the pitch, in the dugout and on the terraces could all agree on was that common sense didn't prevail. I can still hear the song that emanated from all four stands as Steve and I walked off. I won't repeat it here, but it was something along the lines of the referee being a practising masturbator!

I watched the rest of the game in the tunnel. We were not supposed to stand there, but what could the referee do – send me off again? We won the game 2-1 in the end. To their credit, Grimsby managed to get an equaliser before Dwight Yorke scored with 12 minutes to go. Yorkie came off the bench and really looked up for it, so it was no surprise to me that he got the winner.

The gaffer, Ron Atkinson, never said a word to me about me being sent off after the match. I think he knew that it was a ridiculous decision and he was on my side. It didn't stop him calling me over at Bodymoor Heath two days later after training, though. I knew it was coming, and whilst he was sympathetic, I was still fined two weeks' wages. For me, though, the worst part was knowing that I would serve a three-match ban, and in those days it took a few weeks for the ban to come into play. I looked at the forthcoming fixtures and I had a horrible feeling that the ban would start around the time of the fifth round of the FA Cup; we had been drawn away again, and this time it was at Bolton Wanderers. It was going to be a tough game, and I really wanted to play in it. Bruce Rioch was in charge of Bolton, and they were playing really well. Win that match and we were only two rounds from the final. It was a bad game for me to have to miss.

Before this match, though, was the Coca-Cola (League Cup) first leg semi-final game against Tranmere Rovers. That was going to be even harder not to play in – we could almost see the twin towers of the old Wembley.

We had three league games to play before the cup double-header. I took my role as a professional footballer very seriously and believe me, I wanted to play in every game. But I have to be honest, if I had to miss games through suspension, I would have preferred them to have been in the league, as we were so close in the cups and at the time, we were very much mid-table in the league.

As the days after the sending off turned into the first and then the second week, it really did become glaringly obvious that I would be suspended for those cup games. Sure enough, when the FA announced when I would serve my time, it was exactly when I thought it would be. I tried not to show it, but inside I was absolutely gutted. I got the usual back slaps from the lads, and my wife, Carol, was just magic in her support.

I played in two of the three league games before the suspension, a 1-0 home win against Leeds United and a goalless draw, also at home, against Manchester City. I could seek solace in the fact that I had contributed to us not conceding any goals in both of these matches. Professional to the core, me! If I'm not playing, then I am going to be supporting.

Wednesday 16 February 1994
Prenton Park
Tranmere Rovers FC

It's the League Cup first leg semi-final match away to Tranmere Rovers. As I'm suspended, I haven't travelled up with the lads on the coach. Instead, I've got in the car with Carol and a couple of mates.

The build-up to the match was done with all the usual professionalism that I set for myself. I trained just as hard as if I would be playing or at the very least, had a great chance of getting picked. There was no doubt about it – I just had to shut out of my mind the fact that I couldn't play. I knew I'd be available for the return leg, but in the back of my mind I was thinking that if we got thrashed, the last thing I wanted was just to go through the motions at Villa Park. I wanted it to mean something.

I really do hate not playing!

The journey to Prenton Park was just awful, and the weather was atrocious – we half expected to see Noah in his ark with all the animals on the motorway. It really did rain that much!

When we eventually got to the ground, we were taken to the main stand – I guess you can call it the VIP area. Some folk like the kudos of being there, but really I wanted to be the one being watched on the pitch instead of the one watching the game. It made it slightly easier for me, as behind us was Mark Wright. Mark was a good lad who, at the time, was playing for Liverpool in the heart of their defence as well as doing the same for England. I loved the way he played. He was no-nonsense type of defender, and I played in a similar way. I loved it when he scored that goal against Egypt in the 1990 World Cup finals to put us through to the knockout stages. He did it for all of us in that position on the field. He told me that he was looking forward to the match, as he lived on the Wirral and knew some of the Tranmere players and fans. Whilst it was obvious that we didn't share support on who we wanted to win the match, it was really good to be able to chat to him and, to be honest, it took my mind off the fact that I wasn't playing.

The atmosphere in the ground was amazing. I could see the Villa supporters, as they always packed out every away ground they went to, and they were in good voice. I say they were in good voice; the truth is that I couldn't really hear them, as from where I was sitting, they were drowned out by the home fans. But I knew they would be giving as good as they got – they always did.

As the referee blew his whistle to start the match, the roof nearly came off the stand – it was that loud. I remember saying to myself, *Come on, lads. Don't do anything silly. Play to our strengths, and at least take a draw into the second half. We have to still be in the game come the end of these 90 minutes.*

In the end we were still in the game, but it very nearly wasn't the case at all. I thought we were going to take the match to Rovers from the off when Ray Houghton went close but clipped his shot just wide. A couple of minutes later we found ourselves a goal down when Ian Nolan capitalised on a mistake from Steve Staunton and smashed the ball past Bozzie (Mark Bosnich). Then, on the stroke of half-time, Rovers went 2-0 up through Mark Hughes, and this made our job even harder. We badly needed to grab a goal early in the second half. *Come on, boys. You can do this.*

After 78 minutes it was 3-0 to Rovers, fully deserved as well. I couldn't see who scored their goal at first, as all the Tranmere fans were up on their feet begging their team to extend the lead even further, and then they were all dancing in unison. I heard someone shout something about John Aldridge, so I guessed it was him. I put both hands to my mouth. I was shell-shocked to say the least. All I kept on thinking was how the players, my teammates, were feeling there and then. Wembley may as well have been on the moon at the moment in time. It was out of reach, that's for sure!

I looked over at the Villa fans. They were perplexed; they couldn't believe what they were witnessing. Some had seen enough and started to make their way back out to the cars and coaches. They looked like they wanted to be anywhere except where they actually were at that precise time.

I was thinking the same thing, but something told me to stay and see this out. Was there something about to happen to give us hope?

The answer was a big fat juicy *yes*, and it was one of those moments when you get to think that maybe, just maybe, fortune will favour us in the end. The hope was provided with just seconds to go.

We had a free kick taken by Rico (Kevin Richardson) that was headed into the path of Dalian Atkinson, who struck the ball sweetly to make it 3-1. Seconds later it was all over; however, the big man's goal could have changed everything. It gave me a spring in my step as I left the ground, only stopping to shake Mark Wright's hand. He was very pleased but told me that *if* we did go through, we had to beat Manchester United in the final. You just can't beat that northwest rivalry between Merseyside and Manchester! We got back into our car and everyone was talking about Dalian's goal and what it actually could mean in the second leg.

The next day, the conversation was exactly the same in the dressing room as it had been in the car the night before as we assembled for training. Sure, we had lost, but 3-1 was better than 3-0, so we had hope once more. There was a spring in our step that morning, despite the defeat. If I was picked for the second leg, I knew the game would have a meaning that I yearned for.

We had to put it to the back of our minds. We had the FA Cup fifth round coming up on the Saturday, and this was now the focus. I couldn't play again, but I was still professional, and I gave my all in those training sessions and talks before another trip to the northwest to face Bolton Wanderers.

Sunday 20 February 1994
Burnden Park
Bolton Wanderers FC

For the second time in just four days, I'm travelling by car up the M6 with Carol. I am not really used to doing this, as I'm normally on the coach with the rest of the players and the management team. As much as I love Carol, she knows where I would rather be. Joining us is our good friend John Greenfield. We live right by John, and that's how we became good friends with the man who ran the club shop at Villa Park. He would often come round to ours on a Saturday night for a bite to eat and a few drinks. We didn't really go out a lot – it wasn't mine or Carol's thing – but we loved entertaining at home. Not many people know this, but John also managed the videos that were put together after each match. I would always get a copy and then spend hours evaluating the team's performance and in particular mine. It was a really good way to keep tabs on how I could improve.

After a while the conversation in the car switches from what went wrong at Tranmere to what we are going to do to rectify the situation against Bolton. John and Carol make a case to say that the Tranmere disaster wouldn't have happened if I had been playing. This is good to hear of, course, and shows solidarity and support, but it also means that I hate the red card I received against Grimsby even more.

Right now, though, it's all about supporting the lads and at least earning a draw and taking Wanderers back to Villa Park for a replay. Win this game and we are just one away from the semi-finals and more Wembley trips to think about. It's not lost on me that we could be at Wembley three times before the season is out, and if we win the FA Cup, then a fourth beckons in the calendar year in the Charity Shield.

Que sera sera.

There was no way we could take Wanderers for granted, though. They were proving to be giant-killers in the FA Cup, beating Liverpool in it the previous season, and before they played us in the fifth round, they had already knocked out Everton and Arsenal. So as we took our seats at Burnden Park, I felt cautiously optimistic. *Win the game, lads, and I will be able to help us in the next round on the pitch and not cheering off it.*

It was a crisp and cold day, and the BBC had chosen to broadcast it for their live game. At least it wasn't pissing it down as it had been at Tranmere a few days earlier. It was a pretty tight match, and with 10 minutes to go, it looked like we were heading back to Villa Park for a replay, as there had been no goals scored. David Lee had been a little livewire on the flanks all the match for Bolton, and he had decided to cut inside and possibly go for goal when he was bought down by Tony Daley. It was a good 10 to 15 yards outside the box, though, and I felt that it was far enough away not to cause us any real issues. How wrong could I be?

Alan Stubbs had played so well in the heart of the Bolton defence, and it was him who fired a low shot right in the corner of our net. Mark Bosnich got a bit of flak for not being quick enough to get down to the ball. I think this was slightly unfair, as I don't think he saw it with a melee of players in front of him. It was a great strike but a soft goal to concede at the same time.

We had 10 minutes to get back in the game. We huffed and puffed but Bolton were resolute, and we couldn't blow their house down. I recall that there was hardly any injury time, as the referee brought the game to its conclusion bang on the 90-minute mark, and Bolton's remarkable run continued – this time at our expense.

We didn't stay around after the game. We got back to our car quickly for the return journey to Birmingham. It was very strange. On the way up, we had spoken about multiple trips to Wembley, and now we were in serious danger of not getting to play even one game there. Now Tranmere at Villa Park was 'Monte Carlo or bust' for us. I couldn't even think of bust, especially as I could now be selected for the Tranmere game.

There is no time for the players to dwell on this loss, as just two days later, we are playing Manchester City in the league at Villa Park. It's the last game of my suspension. It's a non-starter of a game, really, and it ends without a goal being scored.

Now we have training and I am back in the fold, and all thoughts from everyone turn to Villa Park once more on the Sunday for the second leg of the Coca-Cola Cup semi-final. The pressure is immense in the build-up, not only for us but for the staff and the fans. ITV have chosen it as a live game. The nation will be watching, with the vast majority wanting to see Tranmere, the underdogs, go through.

Sunday 27 February 1994
Villa Park
Aston Villa FC

I'm sitting in the dressing room with the rest of the players. It's close to kick-off, and I can hear the fans in the stands and in their seats. Villa Park is rocking and we can feel it. Team talks are over and it's now time to step up to the plate. I'm back in the team and feel part of this group of players again. We are hungry men who made mistakes and possibly underestimated Tranmere in the first leg, but we are not going to make the same mistake again.

Dean Saunders pulls a goal back in the 19th minute. We are only one goal behind now. Then, four minutes later, this happens.

I'm standing in the opponent's penalty area. I can see the ball coming over to me. It's a great chance to score, but I'm a central defender, so my kick could be a wild one that blazes the ball over the bar. I have to head it, but the cross is low, which makes it hard. Then everything's a blur to me, but luckily not to the local newspaper, the *Birmingham Evening Mail*. This is how they reported what happened next.

> Tranmere were increasingly troubled by angled crosses and their defence vanished like morning mist when Ray Houghton rolled a free kick to Richardson who, from 35 yards away, found Teale plunging in front of Hughes to power a header into the far corner of Nixon's goal. Teale was smiling as he landed.

I am sitting on the pitch, and all I can see is a mass of footballers, wearing claret and blue, diving on and around me. And 40,000 fans begin chanting my name and wildly acknowledging that I have just levelled the tie. Wembley is no longer on the moon – it's crashing back down to earth!

But shortly afterwards, a long ball over the top of our defence has found John Aldridge and the wily old fox has drawn Mark Bosnich to him in the box. The veteran striker is brought down by the defender of his goal. We surround the referee, but we know what the outcome is going to be, as he has already pointed to the spot.

That was bad enough, but what we really didn't want was the subsequent sending off and being down to 10-men with an hour or so still to go. Luckily, after what seems to be an eternity, the referee keeps the red card in his pocket and Bozzie remains on the pitch. I look at him as he does at me, and we both know that it could easily have gone the other way. Aldridge scores from the spot and Rovers have a one-goal lead again. We gee ourselves up as a unit, and at half-time we regroup.

We need one more goal to level the aggregate score, but that third goal isn't coming as the second half commences. It's cat and mouse, and the time seems to go really quickly. Then, in the 88th minute, a pinpoint cross from Tony Daley on the right is met precisely by Dalian Atkinson's head and we are once more on level terms. In my head, I am thinking, *That's it. Extra time it is, then.*

But Tranmere go very close to nicking it when a Liam O'Brien free kick hits the inside of the post, runs behind Bozzie and out the other side. We have survived this and now it really is extra time. I feel emotionally and physically shattered, and I'm not the only one. It's not just us either, but the Tranmere players too. It's a typical extra time period where no one wants to make a mistake and it peters out. No one ever plays for penalties, but it headed that way.

I was the second in line to take a penalty after Deano (Dean Saunders). I wasn't worried at all as I stepped up to take it. Alan Parry was the ITV commentator for the live game, and the co-commentator was Kevin Keegan. This was how Parry described my penalty:

"Right, the man dubbed John Wayne by his manager gets off the horse, ties it up to the post, pulls out the gun. Gets his finger on the trigger and fires the bullet right down the middle."

Kevin Keegan then said that I would have been the first one out of town if I had missed it – John Wayne or not – and then calls it a terrific penalty. Of course, I don't know this at the time, as I am on the pitch. The truth is that the gaffer never called me by this name, but this has since gone down in Villa Park folklore, and I am reminded of it every time I come back. Nice one, Mr Parry!

We eventually win the penalty shootout 5-4 and we have our date with destiny at Wembley. The fans swarm onto the pitch, and we are put on their shoulders. I ran out onto the pitch some two hours before in full work attire, and I leave the pitch in just my underpants. My top and shorts become collector's items for the jubilant Villa fans.

I don't think this will be allowed to happen in the final at Wembley, but for now, on this beautiful day when we have snatched victory from the jaws of defeat, it's just fine.

CHAPTER TWO
Beginnings

I'VE NEVER MET Robin Askwith. You might recall that he was the star of those 1970s soft porn/comedy films that always had a title beginning with the words 'Confessions of...' The first in the series of films was called *Confessions of a Window Cleaner*. He played the window cleaner, and he was always having it away with the housewives – and basically any woman who looked at him. He was also a pop performer, a driving instructor and worked in a holiday camp in later films. They were harmless and very much films of their time. Good fun and very saucy in a British way. I never saw them in the Best Film category at the Oscars.

I'm sure Robin's fellow actors Miranda Richardson and Anthony Quayle have been to the Oscars, as they are both very fine players on the big screen. I never shook hands with either of them either.

I've never met Marc Almond of Soft Cell fame either, and the same goes for Lee Mack, one of our finest comedians today. But I have something in common with all of them – their birthplace. We were all born in Southport, in the northwest of England, although at different times, of course.

Southport lies just off the Irish Sea coast, and the town is 16.7 miles north of Liverpool and 14.8 miles southwest of Preston. For many years it came under the county of Lancashire, but today it's Merseyside. It's a seaside town that has a reputation for being a little more refined than neighbouring Blackpool. Most of the town is only just above sea level. If it rained heavily for a long time, us kids used to think we would be flooded and we'd drown. We learned to swim as quickly as we could walk in those days.

I was born on Tuesday 10 March 1964 at the Christiana Hartley Maternity Hospital, Southport. This makes my star sign Pisces. The hospital was located on Curzon Road and was named after Christiana Hartley, an English social and welfare rights activist, philanthropist and Liberal Party politician. She also became a CBE. I was born in good hands there and to my family in general. Singer Neneh Cherry was also born on this day as well, although not in the same place as I was. I wonder if she knows that she shares her birthday with me?

I was the second child born to Ray and Sylvia Teale. My brother, Mark, was 18 months older than me. At first, we all lived with my nan and grandad in Southport before moving to Warrington. Mum and Dad couldn't settle in the area and so it was back to Southport, where we settled nicely into number 5, Birch Street. It was a good working-class urban area to grow up in. My dad worked at the Ford plant in Ellesmere Port. My mum worked at Mullard, which made electrical components. Mum was also religious, and we were Methodists. She would take us to church every Sunday, but Dad was an atheist. I think he liked the time on his own!

The number one song in the UK when I was born was 'Little Children' by Billy J. Kramer and the Dakotas. Beatlemania was everywhere, not just in the UK but worldwide, especially in the good old US of A. Those formative years were very special, and because we lived so close to Liverpool, we kind of felt part of the Merseybeat scene. *Coronation Street* was also very popular on the TV, and because we lived close to Manchester as well, we soon came to realise that we lived in a very lovely and lucky part of the country.

And making its debut on BBC Two on 22 August 1964 was a programme called *Match of the Day*. It showed football highlights, and the first game broadcast was Liverpool versus Arsenal at Anfield, with Liverpool winning the match 3-2. It sounded like it was a thrilling game, but of course, I would not have remembered it. How could I? I had only been on the planet for 165 days! Football would have meant nothing to me at that time. But as the 1960s made way for the 1970s, all of this was about to change for me.

CHAPTER THREE
Kickabouts and School Days

I DON'T KNOW whether it was fun to stay at the YMCA, but it was certainly fun to play football for them in 1970 at the age of just six. I had been having a kick-around with a lad who lived next door to us in the street. All you had to do was avoid the cars and kick it to each other – standard training back then. The neighbour would have been the same age as our Mark, so 18 months older than me. Still, I enjoyed it because I was starting to get used to having a ball at my feet.

Then, one day, I was invited down to play a game for the local YMCA team. If memory serves me, I was picked to play in midfield. I really enjoyed what I called 'my first serious competitive match'. Remember, I was only six and it meant the world to me. I must have done something right, as I was taken to one side after the game and told that I had played really well. When I was asked if I would like to play regularly for the team, I jumped about as if I had scored the winning goal in the World Cup final!

The World Cup was being played in Mexico that year. I didn't even know where Mexico was then but gathered that it was somewhere in the world, as the cup competition was named after it. I told my mum and dad that one day I was going to play for England, and they were made up for me. They even told me where Mexico was. I couldn't sleep that night because I was that excited. When I did eventually get some shuteye, I dreamt of scoring the winning goal. It didn't matter to me if it was in Mexico or Manchester – just as long as I scored it.

My first manager was a guy called Tony Rimmer. I still see him, and over the years we have become very good friends. We chew the fat and it's always about the game. Back then, he was a big influence on me. He taught me and the rest of the lads to enjoy ourselves and not be afraid of the ball. He taught us to run and pass – not just pass to anybody but to those in a good position or those who could put me into one. Tony was great at teaching us the basics of the game, and at six years of age this meant everything to me. I loved turning out for the YMCA, and this enabled me to get into my school team. I still played for the YMCA, and the more games I played in, the more I enjoyed it and understood the game.

I would still go to Tony Rimmer, even if I wasn't playing for him, and he would offer his advice. Tony talked and I listened. In fairness, I listened to others as well, such as my teachers and my dad, but Tony was the biggest influence on me by far. I was developing physically and mentally in the game, and by the time I had reached the grand old age of nine, I had become a member of Southport Boys team. It was just a natural progression, although the position that I initially played in didn't come naturally to me.

Up to this point, I had played mostly in midfield and occasionally at left back for the YMCA and my school. However, I was picked in goal for Southport Boys – talk about getting to know different departments! I always found being a goalkeeper rather boring and I wanted to play outfield, but I guess I was doing as I was told. My recollections of being the number one were not that great, and it was always freezing and wet.

At that time, there was a film out called *Kes*. It was about a young lad called Billy who came from a dysfunctional family and didn't really fit in at school or at home. That is until he befriends a kestrel that he calls Kes. There is one scene where he is picked to play in goal for his school team, and he spends the time messing about before he is told to go and get a cold shower, and he has no towel with him. Nonetheless, he still has his shower and has to put his clothes back on over his wet body. Now don't get me wrong, I was nothing like Billy in terms of ability, nor did I share his love of birds of prey, but I could relate to this scene from the film because of how cold it was in the dressing rooms and showers. We would all sit on the radiators trying to get warm and then get the old chilblains. I was a bit like Billy from the film, but at least I had a towel!

What was interesting about playing with those lads is that some of us went on to become professionals. One of them was a guy called Andy Mutch, who went on to form a formidable strike partnership with Steve Bull at Wolverhampton Wanderers in the 1980s and 1990s.

If I wasn't playing football or studying at school (yes, I did study!), I would be watching football on TV. We had *Match of the Day* – which was by now well established – on BBC One and it was now shown in colour. Our regional TV station was Granada, and the local commentator was Gerald Sindstat, who sadly passed away a few years back. He was a great commentator, as was John Motson (who passed away in 2023) and Barry Davies, who both featured on *Match of the Day*. They were all so informative, and it came as no surprise when Sindstat joined them on the BBC. To me they were the holy trinity behind their microphones.

One player that always caught my eye was Stuart Pearson, who was known affectionately as Pancho. He was a big bustling centre forward playing for Hull City at the time, although he later earned a big move to Manchester United. His thighs looked massive to me, and I always wanted my thighs to be like his. He also knew where the net was, that was for sure!

As my formative years went by, I started playing in more and more games, and it wasn't uncommon for me to be playing twice on a Saturday and the same on a Sunday. Mum and Dad were usually there together on the touchline cheering me on. If they couldn't both be in attendance, there would always be one or the other.

As if this wasn't enough football, I began playing for a club called Birkdale United at the time that I was playing for Southport Boys. I have really fond memories of playing for this brand-new team that had just been formed. The club was started by Sam and Pat Benbow, and their sons played too. They were such a lovely family. Sam bought a minibus and would pick up and drop off all the lads right outside their doorsteps, so my parents managed to have a rest. We played a lot of games in Liverpool. The Benbows were a dream to all the mums and dads whose kids played football; they were a very well-respected local family in the community.

There was nothing better to me than being out on that pitch. It was my happy place. I didn't hate my school years at all, but the only lessons I loved were the sports ones, whether that was in the school gym or the swimming pool or playing field sports like football and cricket. If you asked me what I was like academically, I would say that I was somewhere in the middle, and the old cliché of 'could do better' would have been apt. However, in sport, I simply excelled.

When I was 11 years old, I went to Birkdale High School. The only lessons that I really couldn't get on with were foreign languages. I tried hard but I just didn't get it, so when it came to choosing my options, these were well and truly ditched.

Whilst I may have preferred to have been selected as an outfield player for Southport Boys, playing in goal did actually bring me my first taste of representing a professional club. In 1977, at the age of 13, I went for trials with Everton. A local scout had heard good things about me from both Southport Boys and Birkdale United. It was while playing for Birkdale that I was actually watched by the scout. I had grown up as an Evertonian, so to get a trial with them meant the world to me. I was only a wee lad, but I vaguely remember their FA Cup win in 1968 and their league title victory in 1970. Everton had some great players at the time, like Colin Harvey, Howard Kendall, Bob Latchford and Joe Royle. Their blue kit looked magnificent on a colour TV as well.

I was so nervous but at the same time very excited as my dad drove me to the trial. I kept on talking all the way there. I must have got on Dad's nerves, but he never showed it. He had got me the trial. He was very friendly with Everton's youth development officer, Ray Minshull, and this was how I came to have the trial. Incidentally, Ray had also been a goalkeeper and had been at Liverpool for a few years during his playing days. His career took him to Southport and Wigan Rovers, and he also coached in Gibraltar and Austria. He was a lovely guy but very much a tough disciplinarian. He was bringing through guys who were just a couple of years older than me – players like Gary Stevens, Steve McMahon and Kevin Ratcliffe. So I knew I was in good hands and good company!

Everton's first thought about me was that I was slightly too small to make it as a goalkeeper, even though I was six foot tall! Later in my career, I was told that I wasn't tall enough to make it in central defence, but that is a story for another chapter.

I soon switched to left back – I guess you can say that I was very much a utility player in those days. It all went according to plan, and just one year later, aged 14 years old, I signed apprenticeship forms at Goodison Park. I felt at home as a Toffee, the club's nickname, playing for my boyhood club. The first team manager at the time was Gordon Lee. He had taken the club to the League Cup final in 1977 before losing to Aston Villa 3-2 in a second replay at Old

Trafford. Replays were the norm in those days if it was all square after the final. Funnily enough, Gordon had played for the Villa as well. It's strange how history can sometimes repeat itself!

This is where I really did start to become independent. I would travel to Everton's training ground every day by bus and train and not rely on lifts from Mum and Dad. The good news was that I was seldom on my own, as there were a group of lads from Southport who had also signed apprenticeship forms, so I had company for the journey to Liverpool. This was where I really did learn my trade. I soon started to clean boots for players like Andy King and John Gidman. If the players wanted sweat suits, we would have to get them and also hang out all their kit. Andy King wore them all the time, God rest his soul. The senior players were an approachable bunch at Everton – so much so that I sometimes got a lift home from the likes of Mick Lyons, who was a great pro and a good bloke. I was soon playing in the B-team and alongside some of those older players that Ray Minshull was bringing through the ranks, such as Kevin Ratcliffe and Steve McMahon. I still see them from time to time today in my local supermarkets, and we also stop and talk about the old days and about our families.

I was enjoying my time at Everton in the late 1970s and the early part of the 1980s. I still didn't think my best position was left back, but I was left footed and strong in that department, so I never complained.

Unfortunately, Gordon Lee was sacked in 1981 and was replaced by fans' favourite (and mine) Howard Kendall. We all know the great impact he was to make in the latter part of the decade, but it wasn't instantaneous on the pitch. Changes were made very quickly off the pitch, and this was where the troubles between me and the club first surfaced.

We were paid £50-a-week as apprentices, and £25 of this would go on digs (paying Mum and Dad) and £10 on travelcards. This meant that I had £15-a-week for myself. Now, this was still a lot of money in those days for a 17-year-old, but the problem was what I did with it.

I lived by the seaside in a popular town for the tourists, and we had plenty of arcades to choose from along the promenade and I started to play them. A lot. So much so that I started to get hooked on them. When my wages had been spent, I would take money out of my savings to feed what was becoming an addiction. My parents were not best pleased with this and neither were the club. In the end, Everton ripped up my contract. I was gutted and realised that I needed a little bit of help, so I went to see a hypnotherapist, and that did the trick. It didn't take long before I was no longer hooked. Looking back, I can see that I was stupid, immature and it was all my own fault. However, because I was so young, I started to hold a grudge against Everton even though in hindsight I can see why they did it. I guess it's all part of learning life and its rich tapestry.

For the first time since I had started to kick a ball at the age of six years old, I was now without a club. This was at a time of rising unemployment as well, and my future looked a little bleak. Fortunately, living where I did meant that there were plenty of odd jobs around, especially in the summertime. Working at the fun fairs and in the arcades and helping out at the local golf courses, such as the Royal Birkdale, was all very good, but I desperately wanted to get back into football.

I started to write to clubs asking for trials. Amongst them were Chester City and Wigan Athletic, and I got offered a trial at Leeds United when Alan Clarke was in charge. He was a legend at the club. In the team was the future Argentina manager Alex Sabella and a very young goalkeeper by the name of David Seaman. We played Huddersfield Town in my trial match, and the following week I got a call from Huddersfield offering me a place in the reserve team. They agreed to pay my expenses, so I joined Huddersfield on a non-contract basis.

It was a great experience, as I got to play at such great grounds as Villa Park and Old Trafford. My experiences playing and training with these professional clubs was a brilliant one. I was playing well in games and was told so, but I wasn't getting the chance to put pen to paper and sign that professional contract that I so desperately wanted. I knew that if I was to succeed, I would have to keep learning and maybe drop down to the non-leagues in order to do so. It wasn't what I wanted, but by then I knew it had to happen. I was going to give it my all in order to achieve my dreams.

As it happened, my non-league journey would take me to clubs closer to home, rather than those across the Pennines that I'd been having trials for. One was even within walking distance of my house!

CHAPTER FOUR
Southport

I ENJOYED MY time at Huddersfield Town, but as great as it was, I still wasn't getting any offers from the bigger professional clubs, and I found myself going back to park football just to keep playing the game I loved.

Then, out of the blue, I received a phone call from someone who suggested that I go and play non-league football. I was so excited that I had received a call to play that I didn't even ask who was calling! If they had given me their name, it simply didn't register – the same was true of the team I was being asked to play for. After a while, I did ask who the club was, but I still didn't ask for the name of the person calling me. As it turned out, it was a manager who went by the name of George Burns. No, not the Hollywood movie star from Tinseltown – a representative of Ellesmere Port football club. This was where my spirits dampened a little, as Ellesmere Port was a good hour or so away and there weren't very good links from where I lived. However, I was told that that there was a player who lived in Formby, and I could get a lift with him.

At that time, I didn't have a driving licence, let alone a car, but I could get a train to Formby, where a bloke called Roger Aindow would pick me up from the station to take me to training and matches and then drop me back off at the station afterwards. He was much older than me and coming to the end of his career. Roger was a central defender who had been on the books of Blackpool and Southport, as well as many other clubs in the northwest of England. Roger had bags of experience and he was very willing to share it with me. Not only were we teammates but we also became very good friends. I played left back for the club and was enjoying myself there once again. I was learning my trade, although I was only getting £25-a-week. It was during one of those car journeys that Roger informed me that there was an opportunity for me to go and play for Southport. They had just taken on a new manager by the name of Bob Murphy. He had built a good reputation as manager of Mossley FC in Manchester in the Northern Premier League, turning them into a very successful club. Southport was one of the 92 teams that were part of the Football League for many years and had only lost their league status in 1978, when they were voted out of the league and replaced by Wigan Athletic. They had recorded three consecutive 23rd-place finishes in the Fourth Division but had been champions of it just a few years before. Southport's decline was a quick one indeed.

Bob came with the reputation of being a hard man and a disciplinarian. Roger told me that it was Bob's way or the highway but if a player had the right attitude and wanted to succeed, there was no one better in non-league football to help them. The idea really appealed to me, and I had a strong feeling that Bob was the man to take me forward into the professional football world. There were a couple of other bonuses as well; I would be earning more money, and Southport's ground, on Haig Avenue, was within walking distance of my home. It was a no-brainer, as I would be playing in a higher league. I would miss Ellesmere Port (I played around 30 games for them, all at left back) and Roger in particular, but I knew I was doing the right thing.

By the start of the 1983–1984 season, I was officially a Southport player. One of our first training sessions was in a gym in Skelmersdale, which was around 20 minutes from Southport. I had not yet met Bob, and we were all there working on our fitness and getting on with things. We didn't see Bob when he arrived, but we certainly heard him. One of the lads, whose name escapes me, was a little knackered by all the physical exertion and proceeded to put both hands on the gym wall for his respite.

"Right," Bob bellowed, "that's a 50p fine. There's no fucking walls on a football pitch!"

That bellowing made us all stop and listen. It was the broadest Mancunian accent I had ever heard, and it was so loud that I would imagine the rest of the staff back at Southport's ground could hear him too! If I had any intention of leaning on a wall in his presence, I can well and truly tell you that there was no way I would from that moment on. Plus 50p was a lot of money to be fined in those days.

Bob knew all about football, so I was very eager to learn from him, but I also knew that he took absolutely no shit from anyone. I was soon picked to play for the team and, as usual, I took the left back perch. We had a useful team, with a guy called Rob Sturgeon at centre half and Andy Mutch up front. We also had a guy named Tony Rodwell in the team. Tony's nephew is Jack Rodwell, who later played for Everton and England. We had a good solid team. There was one occasion when Rob Sturgeon didn't turn up for training. Bob Murphy despised it if players didn't do the basics, like coming to training. The players knew that Rob had picked up a stomach bug at home and this was the reason for his absence. We thought this was a fair and valid reason, but Bob was having absolutely none of it. Bob knew that I was close to Rob and told me, in no uncertain terms, to get him to training. "He can wear a nappy if he needs to," added Bob. We all looked at each other and thought that the gaffer was having us on. Bob had one of those faces that had been 'lived in', and it was pretty obvious by his poker face that he meant every instruction that he had given to me. In the end Rob didn't come in, as he was too poorly.

There was another incident with Rob and the gaffer sometime after that. Rob had broken his nose in a game and had not trained for the week leading up to our next match, which was at home. We had all assembled before the game for some light training and a meal when Rob arrived. Bob walked over to him and enquired ever so politely, "How's your nose, Robert?"

By that time, Rob thought he had the boss onside. "I'm OK thanks, gaffer, and I'm ready to play."

What Rob didn't see was that the boss had a ball in his hand. I had seen this and knew what was coming. Bob launched the ball at Rob's face and bust his nose wide open! Rob wasn't the biggest of blokes and started to squeal in obvious pain. The boss turned round and informed him that he wasn't going to be picked in the match as he had a real busted nose and wasn't fit enough!

Rob was a great golfer, and when he was 16 he was playing off scratch. He had the choice of becoming a pro, but he chose football. At that moment in time, I would have bet my mortgage that Rob regretted that decision.

Nowadays Bob would have been questioned by the police, chucked out of the job and his actions would have been all over social media. But this was the 1980s and it was non-league football. It was brutal. We just sat there open-mouthed!

From my point of view, though, Bob came along at the right time for me. I guess I had been smarting a little from the constant rejections as I tried to break into the professional scene. But going back to non-league and meeting him and Roger was the best thing that could have happened to me at that time. I refocused and worked harder.

As I've said before, Bob took no prisoners, and that list included the chairman of Southport FC – his boss. When there is a fall-out between chairman and manager, there is only ever going to be one outcome. After just one year at the club, Bob was on his way out and was replaced by Bryan Griffiths.

If Bob Murphy looked like he had gone 12 rounds with Muhammed Ali and lived to tell the tale, then Bryan Griffiths would have been the promoter. He was always immaculately dressed and had a bald head and an all-year tan. He was the Jim Smith of non-league football. He brought his son, Rob, with him, a decent midfield player who had been on Liverpool's books. The issue was that Rob wasn't cut out for the non-league scene. He was far too refined for the brutal aspects of football at this level. Bryan brought in a few Scousers that he knew could play at centre back, including George Carr and Ronnie Nadin. They were slightly older than me but knew how to operate at that level.

We were doing OK and holding our own without really pulling up any trees. I guess you could have called us a solid team at that time in the Northern Conference league.

However, we did very well in the FA Trophy. For those who are not familiar with that competition, allow me to explain. It's a competition run by and named after the English Football Association and competed for primarily by semi-professional teams. The competition was instigated in 1969 to cater to those non-league clubs that paid their players and were, therefore, not eligible to enter the FA Amateur Cup.

We had beaten Burscough, Tow Lane and Gateshead in the qualifying rounds to make it three wins on the trot (with no replays). Then we took on Telford United in their own back yard in the first round proper on 21 December. We won 4-2.

We were then drawn against Scarborough, who were one of the better teams in the league above us, the Conference. The second-round tie was held at Scarborough. We were little fancied, but we managed to draw 0-0 to take the game to a replay back at our place. We drew again, 1-1, in the first replay a few days later, at Haig Avenue, with Andy Mutch bagging our goal. We won the second replay by a single goal to nil courtesy of a goal scored by John Owens.

Our reward for this famous scalp was a home draw against an even bigger team in the shape and form of Kidderminster Harriers. With 10 minutes to go, we were winning 1-0 courtesy of Peter King's goal, but the Harriers equalised to earn them a replay.

In February 1986, the country was in the grip of one of its worst winters in years. We thought it might take a few weeks before the replay, but to our amazement we found ourselves travelling down to the West Midlands just one week later. The conditions getting to the ground was just atrocious and it took us hours to get to Kidderminster, even though we set out hours earlier than we would normally have had to. Even driving to Aggborough (Kidderminster's ground), we were convinced the game would be called off. We managed to get to the ground, and the first thing we did was check out the pitch. It was rock hard, almost like concrete in places and an ice-skating rink in others. We knew there was no way this game would be played; we were just waiting for the referee to confirm it. From the pitch, we made our way to the dressing room, or, as we called it, 'Ice Station Zebra', where we discovered that, to our utter amazement, the referee deemed the pitch playable. *Who for, Torvill and Dean?*

It's fair to say that the Harriers adapted to the conditions a lot quicker (and better) than we did. We were one down within the first minute, and everything they did from that moment on seemed to result in more goals for them. In their team was Paul

Davis, who had played for England at semi-professional level, and they had players like Kim Casey as well. Kim was a great player, and he actually turned down the chance of joining West Ham United to stay at the Harriers. In those days, non-league players had full-time jobs – I was a painter and decorator – and Kim earnt more from his job than West Ham were offering him, so he'd have had to take a pay cut to join the Hammers. Incidentally, West Ham finished in the top three of the First Division in the 1985–1986 season.

When the referee blew the whistle to end the first half, the score was:

Kidderminster Harriers 5 Southport 0

We trundled sheepishly into the dressing room and Bryan Griffiths stood there with steam coming out of his ears. To say he was furious was an understatement. Brian's number two was Dave Jones, who had played for the likes of Everton, Coventry City and Preston North End and went on to have a very good career in management with Stockport County, Southampton, Wolves, Cardiff and Sheffield Wednesday. Dave also wasn't best pleased with us, but it was nothing to how Brian was. I sat down to have a slurp of tea and for some reason, I started to mutter under my breath that it was a waste of time being mad at us now, as the game was over. Brian heard this and stopped ranting, came up to me and with the palm of his hand smashed my cup into my teeth, breaking a few of them in the process. I didn't feel the initial pain because I was now seeing a red rag in front of me. I did no more than get up and pick Brian up. I remember that his feet were dangling as I was just about to land a punch on him. Luckily, Dave Jones had pre-empted the strike and held me back. To this day, I thank Dave for doing that. I just lost it, and I honestly don't think I would have stopped at just one punch either. My career in football would have been finished before it had really begun, and my dreams of making it as a professional would have been forever lost. Cheers, Dave!

We lost 6-1 in the end.

It was the second season on the trot that we had exited the cup following a big thrashing. The season before, it had been at the hands of Worksop Town in the second qualifying round. At least we had gone much further this time around.

I knew that what had happened in the dressing room would cost me my place and that I would be suspended. In the end I served a three-week ban. When I returned to the fold, I didn't play initially. Brian's mind seemed to be well and truly made up. It took a few weeks for things to settle down between us, but I eventually got back into the team as left back.

We had an away game at Goole Town and Brian pulled me to one side in the dressing room. My initial thought was *What have I done now?* All sorts of things went through my mind. I must have gone through a thousand scenarios of what it could be about: some were positive, others were not. However, one scenario that wasn't going through my head was that Liverpool – the English champions – were interested in taking me on trial. That's exactly what Brian told me. I was stunned, and silence hung in the air for a short while. Before I had the chance to respond, Brian told me that he had no idea why they wanted me, as I wasn't really good enough. Thanks, Brian! Obviously things between us hadn't settled down as much as I had thought. After that, I lost all respect for him. Of course, I wasn't about to turn down the opportunity to join the Anfield club, and so on the Monday morning, I reported to Liverpool's training ground at Melwood.

I was there for the first week and things were progressing nicely. I was told that I would be picked for the next few reserve matches. These were generally played in mid-week, and therefore I would be getting my Saturdays back. Then I was told that I couldn't be selected, as Southport wouldn't change my contract to allow me to turn out for Liverpool's reserves. I thought this was really strange. They had allowed me to train with Liverpool but wouldn't let me play for them. I was disappointed but thought it would be resolved the following week. But it wasn't. In the end, in the weeks I was at the club, I played just one match for Liverpool's second string, and they released me without offering me a contract. Was I disappointed? You bet I was, but overall, what an experience it had been.

It was great to be surrounded by such a wealth of talent, and I got to know some of the first-team players like Alan Hansen,

Kenny Dalglish and Mark Lawrenson. It was not uncommon of them to give me a lift home at times. Kenny was actually player/manager then. I got the train from Southport to Hillside, which wasn't too far from Southport. It was a beautiful area and where some of the pros lived. Mark Lawrenson actually lived next door to the station, and I would often go to his house to get a lift to training. They were some of the best players in the world playing for *the* team, but they were so genuine and down to earth. I never took it for granted either. They, and my parents, kept my feet on solid ground. Which was a good job, because the last place I wanted to go back to was Southport.

There was an eventual parting of the ways when I was sold to Northwich Victoria for a fee of £2,500 shortly after my trial at Liverpool. They were based in Cheshire, so it wasn't that far for me. OK, it wasn't quite walking distance like it was at Southport, so I would have to use public transport once more, but they were in the division above Southport, so I didn't mind the travel.

Victoria's manager at that time was a guy called Cliff Roberts. There were just eight games left of the season, and it looked to all intents and purposes like they would be relegated. My mantle was an easy one when I spoke to Cliff, and that was to help the club stay in the Vauxhall Conference League. It was going to be an almighty uphill task, but Cliff convinced me that we could do it and I was up for the challenge. It wasn't just me either, because Cliff brought in a sweeper called Stuart Parker. Stuart had been around the non-league scene in the northwest for some years. He was about 33, so much older than me, but he wasn't the oldest player who was brought in. That accolade went to Gordon Hill. Gordon had made his name playing for Manchester United on the left wing and had also represented England at full international level. It was clear that Northwich were going for it and doing everything they could to avoid the drop.

If Dave Jones had saved my career at Southport, the move to Northwich Victoria changed it. Cliff had a vision that he wanted the team to change tactics and play three at the back. I was played on the left-hand side of that three, so I moved from left back to centre half. I took to it like a duck to water.

We had eight games to right the wrongs. And that is exactly what we did, winning six, drawing one, losing just once, and we avoided the drop by finishing in 17th place. Perhaps our best win during that period was away at Weymouth, who were one of the division's big hitters. It was the game where we really started to believe we could stay up.

It was a great feeling on the last day of the season when survival was confirmed. Cliff Roberts had played a blinder bringing in the players that he had done.

We started the 1988–1989 season in fine style by winning two out of the first three games, and that meant we were now in the top half of the table. Shortly afterwards, I took a phone call from Cliff. I had heard that scouts had been to those games and I was potentially being earmarked for a favourable move. At the time, it was just rumours and nothing concrete had occurred in terms of bids, but in the back of my mind I was really hoping that, if true, I would be offered a chance to play in one of the professional leagues. When I did get the call from Cliff, he informed me that the club had received a bid for me. I thought I was going to make it to the promised land, but as it happened, it wasn't a league club at all. Instead it was one of the best and most progressive clubs in non-league – Weymouth. I was told to call their manager, Stuart Morgan, to see what the offer was and then call Cliff back for further advice as to whether I should move or not.

The conversation with Stuart, my potential new boss, made me feel that I would get on with him. So far, so good. Then we started to get down to business. I was offered a three-year contract at £150-per-week, a club house and a £2,000 signing-on fee. Now, at Northwich Victoria, I was on £45-a-week with absolutely none of the other incentives that were being offered. I thanked Stuart and said I would get back to him.

True to my word, I called Cliff back to relay the terms and ask for his advice. I knew a lot depended on what my current boss was about to tell me, so I waited with bated breath. There was a lot to tell him, and I thought I would start with what my weekly wage would be. I told him, and without any hesitation he said, "See you, Shaun." I hadn't even told him about the house and the signing-on fee, and he told me he didn't want to hear any more!

My boss was telling me, in no uncertain terms, to sign for Weymouth, and I really liked the idea. However, I would have to relay everything back to someone who would ultimately make the final decision – *the boss*, if you like – my wife and partner in crime, Carol.

CHAPTER FIVE
Carol
By Carol Teale

HAVING EIGHT BROTHERS and a football-mad father meant football was never that far from conversation at the dinner table or in front of the TV. Southport was a place where everyone seemed to know each other and the local team was the focal point of the community.

My profession was nursing, and I had worked in the USA before coming back home. In those days, a lot of us had second jobs, and I worked at some of the local bars pulling pints for the locals and the holidaymakers. You can imagine how busy that was in the summer period.

I got to know someone called Mavis Clapham, who was married to Southport football club's chairman, Charlie. I bumped into Mavis in the town one day in 1985. She asked me if I would help out behind the bar for a forthcoming event at the club after a game, where the players would be there as well as the fans. I told her I would be happy to help out. I turned up for my shift and was told we would be in for a busy night. I could hold my own with football talk, but I must admit I didn't know much about the Southport players. In fairness I was too busy behind the bar to even look up at them to take any notice, although, unbeknown to me, one of the players had noticed me. The event started to die down a little and I was allowed to finish a little earlier than I had expected, so I decided to stay and have a drink myself. I sat down with Mavis and some of the other staff and we spoke about how well the evening had gone and we had a good laugh. I was just starting to think about going home when I felt a tap on my shoulder. I turned around to see this bloke with a cute face and a cheeky grin. I didn't know what to say, but he did, and it was a good job, because he broke the ice with a classic 1980s chat-up line. "Am I taking you out tonight?" he said.

My initial thought was *What a cheeky bugger. You don't even know me.*

Mavis was knocking my leg as if to offer encouragement for me to say yes, but I did nothing more than smile and go to the toilet. When I came back, the cheeky bloke had moved away from our table. Mavis and the girls were all saying something like, "Do you know who he is? He's a Southport player called Shaun Teale. Why don't you say yes?"

What I hadn't realised at the time was that Shaun had been playing darts with the fans, and he had turned around to one of them and said that he would be taking the barmaid out. Apparently, one of the fans had asked him to point out which one he was talking about, so Shaun obliged. The fan replied, "That's my sister you fancy, then." Shaun was actually talking to my brother, Ronnie Smith. Talk about fate!

Soon afterwards, Shaun was back at the table and we were just chatting. I must admit he made me feel very comfortable, and I was happy to be in his company. At the time, I had my own place but had arranged to go to my parents' house for something to eat. I told Shaun that he couldn't come in and that he would have to wait an hour or so for me to finish my tea. He agreed to wait, and he said he would meet me over the road under the streetlamp.

While we had our family meal, I was thinking that he wouldn't be waiting for me and had decided to leg it. I didn't know it at the time, but while we were eating, the heavens opened and it poured with rain. It was only when I opened the door that I realised how bad the weather was, and when I looked across the road, there was Shaun waiting for me. He was soaked through. I only lived a couple of minutes away, so I told him he could come back and dry off. I thought it was so lovely that he had waited for me in that awful weather. It was the least I could do for him.

When we got back to my house, he asked if he could use the toilet, and when he came back down the stairs, he said that he didn't feel too good. The mixture of the drinks at the club and being out in the rain had knocked him about. I had a breakfast bar in the kitchen and I told him to strip down to his briefs and I would wash his clothes for him. I made him something to eat while his clothes dried, and he began to feel much better. Shaun insisted that he took me out to say thank you for what I had done for him.

Shaun did take me out, and it turned out to be a fabulous first date and we got on really well. At the end of the evening, we both jumped into a taxi, and when we got to mine, he asked if he could come in. I was on an early shift at the Promenade Hospital and I told him it wouldn't be a good idea, but he just gave me one of his cheeky grins and I agreed that he could come in – "Just for coffee." We continued chatting and getting to know each other, and he then cheekily told me that he would stay the night. I called him "a cheeky bugger" and reiterated that I had my shift in a couple of hours. I told him I would make up a bed for him and he just started to laugh. I asked him what he was laughing at, and he told me with an even bigger grin that he was getting into bed with me! He did it in such a lovable, roguish way. I told him he could but to keep himself over the far end of the bed.

He was such a gentleman and I felt totally relaxed in his company – so much so that I left him sleeping in my bed while I went to work. I had only met him a few hours earlier, but it all felt right. He became a permanent fixture at my house straight away. I got to know his family and vice versa. It felt so natural being with him.

Needless to say, Shaun officially moved in on Christmas Day 1985. It was our first Christmas together, but for the actual meal on the 25th, we had agreed that we would have dinner separately. As well as having eight brothers, I also had four sisters, so the Smith household was full to the brim. However, it meant it would give us something to look forward to on Boxing Day, when we could spend as much time together as we wanted.

Shaun had his Christmas Day dinner with his parents and his brother, and just as I was leaving my parents' house, the phone rang. It was Shaun. I asked him if he'd had a good day with his folks. He told me he had ended up in a fight with his dad and had walked out and wouldn't be going back. I told him to meet me at my house. He pulled up in a taxi and asked me for the money for it, as he had left the house in a right rage, in a hurry and without his wallet. He basically turned up in the clothes he had been in all day. Luckily he had some clothes at mine in any case, and that was the start of us living together.

Unfortunately, it took him a few years to step back into his mum and dad's house after that episode on Christmas Day. By that time, we had settled down and had a couple of kids. Nathan was born on 30 June 1987 and Ryan was born on 3 June 1988. They almost looked like twins, and we were asked a few times whether they were. We didn't actually get married until 20 June 1990.

So in less than three years we had met, moved in together and had our children. Some people take a lot more time to get to that position, but our lives were meant to be, and it didn't matter to us in terms of timing. We were (and still are) a very strong couple. We're still in love, still getting on each other's nerves but still together, and that is the most important thing.

The big difference, though, is that we don't have to move around anymore so that Shaun can play football. I knew what I was getting myself into when we got together, and to be honest, I embraced it. Shaun would live out his dream and I would support him and raise the family. I loved it and I wouldn't change a thing. We both got what we wanted, and we worked hard for it. Our first major move was from Southport to Weymouth, where we swapped the north for the south, so that was a major challenge.

We made a great team ourselves!

CHAPTER SIX
Weymouth

WHEN I SIGNED for Weymouth, the club put me up in a nearby hotel and I spent the first week or so on my own. I had never been away from Carol and the boys for this long before, but the good news was that the football stopped me getting into a pickle over it. I signed for the club on the Friday and the following day we had a game away at Boston United. I put all my efforts into getting to know my new teammates and understanding the manager's methods.

It was a very interesting time to play for Weymouth or, indeed, follow them. The club had sold its ground to Asda for a reported deal worth £8 million and had moved into a purpose-built new ground on the outskirts of the town. Looking back now, they were probably the first club to do this, but it's happened a lot since. The stadium had a capacity of nearly 7,000 and had a new state-of-the-art training pitch next to it. We were the envy of non-league football, and no doubt some teams in the lower echelons of the Football League were also casting envious glances in our direction. There would be no chilblains and sitting on radiators for me or the other players with this lot. It was just brilliant.

To celebrate the new stadium, Manchester United came to play us. The ex-West Ham United and England manager, Ron Greenwood, unveiled the stadium prior to kick-off. United were managed by Alex Ferguson (he hadn't been knighted by then), and players such as Bryan Robson, Remi Moses and Norman Whiteside lined up for the Red Devils. Incredibly, we won the game 1-0. I had only been there a few weeks, so that result was just amazing.

It felt really good being part of the team knowing that great players such as Andy Townsend, Graham Roberts, Trevor Sinclair and Tony Agana had played for the club before making the journey into the Football League. I had played my first home game and the club had welcomed me into the matchday programme – and informed everyone that I was also available for professional painting and decorating work outside of my Weymouth commitments!

So those first 11 days had gone well, and I had settled down as much as I could, but it was time to get the family down from the north to the south. I caught the train back home so I could help out with the packing, but Carol, being Carol, had already done the vast majority of it. We packed the van up with the help of Carol's sister and brother-in-law, Nita and Les. We shut the doors on our place and made sure the family would keep an eye out on it. Nita and Les did the driving, because at that time neither of us actually drove. We made sure our sons were comfortable for the journey and off we went to seek out new adventures down south. Nathan was 13 months old and Ryan was just six weeks. Of course, there had been tears from family members up north, but the support was amazing and the reasons we were moving were fully accepted.

It took us a fair few hours to get to our new home, and it was such a relief when we opened the front door. It had two bedrooms and was pretty spacious. We lived in a place called Upwey. Straight away we immersed ourselves in the area, and we started to plan for the future by identifying the best nurseries for the kids to attend. The buses from Upwey to and from the town centre were regular, so we were able to explore Weymouth really well. The beach was great, as was the harbour. All in all, it was a lovely place to live.

I also started to get noticed in terms of my decorating skills, as I was taken on by a lovely guy called Gary Borthwick. Gary had played for the club himself and was very well known and popular in and around town.

My playing position was still centre half, and I was really enjoying this new challenge. The difference between playing for Northwich Victoria compared to Weymouth was that I was used to playing as part of a three across the back at my former club. Stuart was a more traditional 4-4-2 type of manager, and I was now playing in a more recognised and familiar system. I played alongside a good guy called Paul Compton, who had played in the Football League for Torquay United. Paul was a big strapping lad who took no prisoners. I was content that I was still learning my trade and had experienced different systems.

We hit the ground running in the league, and we were one of the best teams in the Conference, along with Barnet, who were managed by Barry Fry at that time. We had possibly the best goalkeeper in the league as well in Peter Guthrie. He was a fellow northerner – I was from the northwest and he was from the northeast – but he was a really good Geordie lad who had moved down at a similar time to me. Peter had made several world-class saves in the game against Manchester United, which got him noticed by other clubs, and it came as no surprise when he joined up with Tottenham Hotspur sometime later.

We had a good mix of lads from all over the country in that team, and the blend was just right. Promotion to the Football League was starting to look like the real deal – perhaps Weymouth would not have to be a stepping stone for me after all.

However, just as we started to get a little excited, our hopes of winning promotion sank without a trace – or rather the pitch did! It turned out that our new ground had been built on a flood plain, and when the heavens opened, it flooded the pitch and the training ground. The powers that be informed the club that to honour the fixtures, while we couldn't use our ground, we would have to play away. We thought the flooding issue would clear up after a couple of weeks, so we were not overly bothered. However, the flooding worsened, and one or two matches became several weeks.

Weymouth is a coastal town, and it meant that our long journeys all over the country by coach took its toll on us, especially with most of us (if not all) having jobs outside the game. Sometimes, key players could not make the game, but I was lucky in that I was working for someone who had played football, and Gary always allowed me the time off. The issue was that we were being pulled all over the place, and in the end, it caught up with us all – we were picking up injuries, mainly through the fatigue caused by travelling.

As quickly as we had marched up the league to challenge the likes of Barnet, we found ourselves slipping down it, and in the end, we finished 10th. It was so disappointing given that we had a magnificent stadium where everything from the goalposts to the corner flags was brand new and we had a state-of-the-art training ground. Don't forget that we had also beaten the mighty Manchester United in a game as part of our great start to the season. We lost 14 games away and only one at home, and that in itself tells the story.

In the end, there was disappointment for Barry Fry and his Barnet team too, as they finished runners-up to the eventual champions, Lincoln City. Lincoln had been relegated from the Football League the previous season, so it was a very quick return for them. We actually took four points from Lincoln, which shows how good we were, but that was little consolation for us. We beat them 3-0 at home and came away with a point at Sincil Bank. Only two other teams had stopped the champions-elect from scoring on home soil. We would have preferred to have given them the points and swapped places, but that's life and that's football for you.

From a personal point of view, I was happy with my contribution over the season. You can always judge this by the fans' reaction, especially when you live in a town and a close community like Weymouth. If you are having stinkers or have the wrong attitude, a footballer will generally not get acknowledged on the street or fans won't buy you a drink at the bar. I managed to get both, so I knew I was doing something right. During the whole of my career, I always wore my heart on my sleeve when I played, and I think the fans of the clubs I played for appreciated that.

As we moved into the 1988–1989 season, it appeared that we were nursing a hangover from our poor end to the previous campaign. We struggled to get into any sort of rhythm and found ourselves near the foot of the table from an early stage. Forgive the pun, but the whole flooding fiasco seemed to have dampened the spirits within the club. We had brought in a couple of new players during the close season. Sometimes they gel and sometimes they don't, but unfortunately for us, it was the latter, and their arrival upset the balance of the side. Again, from a personal point of view, I was happy with my performances during that season, but knowing this wasn't the case for the rest of the team overshadowed it somewhat for me.

Nevertheless, the club had informed me that they were going to enter into talks with me about a new contract. At that same time, there were rumblings that Stuart was under pressure from the board, and as a result, there was a strange feeling around the club. Stuart was a very popular manager amongst the players and the staff in general. OK, results were not going our way and we had the flood issues from the previous season, but he was the type of person that we knew could get us out of the mess we'd found ourselves in. It was certainly not the lost cause that the atmosphere around the club suggested. Then one night, I was having a drink with Stuart in one of the local bars and he informed me that Bournemouth were interested in signing me. I nearly dropped my pint and said, "Bournemouth? From the Football League?"

Stuart laughed and replied, "Yes, *that* Bournemouth."

My heart started to race at the news. There was no way I could turn down the opportunity of fulfilling my ambition, but at the same time I was just about to enter into new contract talks with Weymouth. I felt I owed them, so out of respect I listened to Weymouth's offer.

When I was formally told of Harry Redknapp's interest in taking me to Bournemouth, I was allowed to go to Dean Court (the home of Bournemouth back then) and speak to Harry and Brian Tiler. Brian was an ex-Aston Villa player who was on the board of the Second Division club. The talks went well and I liked what I heard – as did Carol – so I went back to Weymouth and told the club of my intention to sign for Bournemouth. They agreed to it, but only if I was allowed to play one more game for Weymouth, an FA Trophy match against Newport County. Bournemouth duly agreed and parted with £50,000 to acquire my services. That figure could rise to £100,000 depending on the number of games I played, if we won promotion to the First Division and if I played for England. I became the second Weymouth player to sign for Bournemouth that decade after Paul Morrell's move some six years previously.

Ironically, Stuart himself joined Bournemouth as chief scout a few months later. This did not go down well with Weymouth or the fans. It was perhaps a transfer too far after I had left them so recently. There had been some pride in the way that both clubs treated each other.

So, at the age of 24, I could now call myself a professional footballer. I had learned my trade the hard way in non-league, and although at times I had taken two steps backwards to take one forward, I never moaned about it or thought *Oh, woe is me.* My attitude and sheer determination had carried me through, always keeping my eyes on that professional prize.

Cliff Roberts had been correct when he had told me that Weymouth was the right move to get me where I wanted to be. I loved my time there, and that first season when we moved into that new stadium and when we played Manchester United are some of my best memories in football. The people at the club and around it were great for me. I had given them my best and it had paid off.

Now it was time to do it with another club on the south coast and to be paid full-time for it as well. I signed a three-year contract at Bournemouth with a signing-on fee of £15,000, and I was now on £300-a-week. We moved from Weymouth into a club house in Southbourne on the Over Cliffe. Carol and the kids loved the new place, even though we were a little sad to leave Weymouth and the friends we had made there. We were still in Dorset, so we could still see anyone that we wanted to keep in touch with.

The challenge to myself and to the club was well and truly on.

CHAPTER SEVEN
AFC Bournemouth

MY FIRST EVER game as a professional footballer took place on 4 February 1989, a home match against West Bromwich Albion in the Second Division. I wasn't expecting too much first-team action when I joined the club just a few weeks before, but Harry (Redknapp) assured me that it wouldn't take long. I was a substitute for the game, and I recall taking my seat in the dugout and thinking that I was now a professional footballer. Even though I desperately wanted to get on the pitch, I savoured every moment.

The crowd that day was just shy of 12,000. I sat there taking it all in, but deep down I had a feeling that I would get onto the pitch. Kevin Bond was playing in my position. He had been a good servant to the club, but the son of the former Manchester City and Norwich City boss, John Bond, had major issues with his hip and was due for major surgery that would possibly mean him missing the rest of the season. In those days, squad rotation wasn't a thing, and basically if a player was out due to injury, he would be in real danger of not getting back in if the replacement was playing well. You could tell it was niggling him, and the more the match progressed, the more it took a hold of him. Then, with half an hour to go, Harry turned to me and told me to warm up, as I would be replacing Kevin. "Yes, boss," I replied without even thinking too much about it. I was ready for this day. I'd been ready for nine years.

I duly replaced Kevin and took my position on the left-hand side in the centre of our defence. Let battle commence – and commence it did. I got stuck in and showed no fear of the Albion attack. We won the game 2-1. I wasn't just over the moon, I circumvented it around 20 times! I got pats on the back from my teammates and more importantly from Harry. The next morning, we took the kids into the town centre and Carol and

I must have bought every national and local paper, searching desperately for the match report, with big smiles on our faces whenever we saw my name mentioned.

The following Saturday was another red-letter day for me, as I made my full debut away at St Andrew's, the home of Birmingham City. There was no way I was going to get complacent. I had worked too hard to let that happen, so I knew I had to be at my best. We won the game 1-0. As a central defender, not conceding a goal was all I could ask for, but what really made me happy was my performance. No way did it feel like my first full game as a professional footballer; it felt like I'd played hundreds. This is not meant to sound cocky by any stretch of the imagination, but I just felt at home on the pitch. It was the only place I wanted to be – right in the thick of it. To top off a great day, I won the Man of the Match award. Suffice to say that our local newsagent was happy with me and Carol once more, as we bought every paper that we could.

The highlight of the day, though, was that Ray Harford had been at the match and had been quoted as saying that this was one of the best full debuts he had ever seen. Under his guidance, Luton Town had won the League Cup the previous year and were on their way to reaching the final once more. This was high praise indeed.

I still have the match report cutting written by Peter Robinson, who was the *Bournemouth Echo* correspondent:

> Shaun Teale passed his first full test in the Football League with flying colours.

The article included a quote from my manager, Harry Redknapp:

> I thought he did incredibly well. He was outstanding, quite incredible for someone playing his first game in the league. He never looked like making a mistake.

I also made comments about the team we had played that day:

> No question, I'm going to meet better teams than this in the Second Division. They were a poor side, and there are

going to be much better people than that I'm going to have to deal with in the future.

It may have been my first full game for Bournemouth, but I know these comments would have also delighted the team I would join afterwards!

The Bournemouth team that started the match on my full professional debut was:

Goalkeeper: Gerry Peyton.
Defence: Mark Newson, Paul Morrell, Shaun Teale, John Williams.
Midfield: Sean O'Driscoll, Richard Cooke, David Coleman, Trevor Aylott.
Attack: Ian Bishop, Luther Blissett.

Two games in and I had a perfect record. Then the football gods seemed to conspire against me, as our next game was an FA Cup fourth-round match at Dean Court against none other than the mighty Manchester United. There was a real buzz leading up to the match, as Bournemouth had defeated United in a third-round clash some five years before with Harry in charge. The score that day was 2-0, and what made this even more special was that United were the FA Cup holders at the time.

The town and the club were buzzing during the week leading up to the game. Training was even more intense. However, the issue for me was that I had played in a previous round for Weymouth, and this meant I was cup-tied. I was gutted, as I had loved playing against United for Weymouth. So I had to watch from the stands and cheer on my new teammates.

Dean Court was packed to the rafters and we managed a credible 1-1 draw against Alex Ferguson's team, but we lost the replay at Old Trafford 1-0. What made it even worse was that the only goal was scored by one of our own players when Sean O'Driscoll put the ball into our net. The lads had put up a good fight in both games, but alas, we couldn't match the team of 1984.

I was on the coach with the players going to Manchester. It was a great experience and another chance to experience more professional activities and get to know my new teammates.

Kevin Bond's worst fears came true when it was officially announced that he would be out for the rest of the season. It turned out that he would need a piece of bone inserted into his hip. As much as I felt for Kevin, I knew that his absence would give me an opportunity to cement my place in the team. Even though we were sitting comfortably in mid-table, I knew that I could never get complacent. It wasn't in my DNA. But Kevin's long-term layoff meant that I could enjoy my football even more and soak it all up. The added bonus was that I was playing in a back four that was very experienced in this division, and I knew I could learn from them all. We had Gerry Peyton in goal, Peter Morella at left back, Mark Newson on the right and big John Williams alongside me in the centre.

We eventually finished that season in a very respectable 12th place, 20 points from the relegation zone and just 12 from the playoffs. The overriding feeling was that we could have done much better. We had faded in the second half of the season, and after that win at Birmingham, we won five, drew four and lost nine. A few more victories and we might have been up there, but overall, I couldn't complain. I had played the first 20 games of my professional career and loved every minute of it. What made some of those even better was working with my old Weymouth manager, Stuart Morgan, again. With Stuart and my teammates and under the guidance of the experienced Harry Redknapp, I knew I had done the right thing in joining the Cherries. And now it was time to stop reflecting and look forward to my first full season as a professional footballer.

Carol, the kids and I had settled well in our new surroundings in Dorset. We were still in the club house at the Over Cliffe. The summer of '89 was a good one. We almost had our own private beach, we were that close to the sea. The four of us were always on it, and we always took friends and family there. When we started pre-season training, I always met the family afterwards on the beach. It was idyllic and just a wonderful time for us all.

My relationship with Harry at that time was a good one. He offered me a pay rise of another £50-per-week, which I was very happy to accept, of course. What I didn't realise at the time, and it can be classed as naivety, was that another year was added to my contract.

Pre-season training for the forthcoming 1989–1990 season had gone well. Kevin Bond had recovered from his hip operation, which was great for him and for the squad, but I had made the position my own and I had no intention of giving it up. Still, it would keep me on my toes.

We started the season brightly and once again found ourselves in a mid-table position and more than capable of pushing ahead and reaching for the playoffs at the very least. We won five games, drawing three and losing four. We had memorable home wins against Hull City and Newcastle United. We had picked up 18 points. Our next 12 league matches took us up to the end of the 1980s, but we only picked up 11 points from this round of games, and whilst we didn't occupy any of the relegation places, we knew there would have to be improvements as we said hello to the new decade.

Things did improve for us in the first couple of months of 1990. After losing 2-0 to Sheffield United in the third round of the FA Cup, we remained unbeaten in the league until 28 February, when Newcastle United took revenge on us for their earlier beating at Dean Court. We had won three and drawn three before this defeat. Again, it had pushed us away from the drop zone and into mid-table, and once again, thoughts turned to maintaining our form and maybe getting into the playoffs. That was going to be our sole focus from now until the end of the season.

And then, in true football fashion, the walls that harboured our hopes and dreams came crashing down around us, for the team and for me personally.

We didn't win a league game for almost two months, picking up just four points. In fact, we lost four games on the trot in April – home losses versus Swindon Town and Leicester City in between defeats on the road at West Ham United (the team Harry Redknapp had played for) and Plymouth Argyle. Instead of looking to the playoffs, we now found ourselves in the bottom three with just three games remaining. We won the first of these to give ourselves some hope, but defeats in our last two games condemned us to plying our trade in the Third Division. In reality, we won just one of our final 16 games of the season with 11 defeats, so we only had ourselves to blame.

And what about my performances for the club during this period when we just fell apart? What about my contribution? My season was over just a few games into this depressing run, so my performances and contributions came in the dressing room and from the terraces. I quickly understood just how Kevin Bond had felt when I was ruled out for a long time. Unlike Kevin, I wasn't missing because of my hip.

On 10 March 1990, we played away at Vale Park, home of Port Vale. Any thoughts of being involved in a relegation dog fight were the furthest thing from our minds as we took to the pitch, as was the fact that this would potentially be my last game of the season.

We drew the game 1-1. It was a tough match and the boys dug in, and the draw was a fair result in the end. Harry was pleased with the performance and told us all to relax for the rest of the weekend and said he would see us for training on Monday morning.

So Monday came around and we reported for training. There was nothing out of the blue about the session. What was, though, was Harry informing us that we would have a practice match and it would be a full 11-a-side. This was something that did not happen very often. None of the players questioned it, though, as Harry and the coaching staff picked the two teams. On the opposite side to me was Paul Moulden. Paul had previously played for Manchester City and had been a tough but prolific goal scorer. He had experienced a stop/start type relationship with Bournemouth, though, and found himself in and out of the team. This must have affected him, as he found the goals became harder to come by. He had been left out of the team that had picked up that point at Port Vale, and he wasn't very happy with that. Perhaps he had a point to prove.

The practice match kicked off, and soon both Paul and I found ourselves going for a 50/50 challenge. It was all routine stuff, but Paul went through me like the proverbial bull in a china shop. I knew something serious had happened straight away, as my kneecap just popped. I knew there was serious damage, but the strange thing was that at that moment in time I felt absolutely no pain. Because of this, I was told to go home and somebody from the medical side at the club would be in touch. I was driving by then, but I only ever drove automatics, which was good news, as the damage had been done to my left knee.

It was only after I got home that the real problems started. Almost as soon as I walked into the house, my left knee began to swell – and that was when the pain hit me. I eventually got the call from the club's medical team, and I informed them that it had got worse. I was immediately told to go to a local hospital called Lansdowne, where a surgeon would take a look at it. However, I had to drive there myself, as Carol wasn't driving at that time. Can you imagine a player having to do this now?

I was greeted at the hospital by a doctor called John Dinley, and he explained to me what the procedure would be. If I needed surgery, he would be my surgeon. My worst fears were about to be confirmed, as he told me that I had snapped the ligaments in my left knee. It was wobbling all over the place as I lay on the couch, and the pain was horrendous. Within a couple of hours, I was in theatre having an operation. I was really lucky that the hospital had reacted so positively, as it meant it could be dealt with straight away and not allow for any further deterioration of the knee. When I woke up after the surgery, I found myself in a private room wearing a plaster cast on my left leg, with Carol sitting by me. It felt so strange having it on. One of the first things that happened was a nurse telling me that I could not leave the bed and if I needed the toilet, a bed pan would be provided. There was no way I was having that and decided I needed to spend a penny. This was when I fully realised just how right the nurse was and how heavy the actual plaster cast was. I swung my leg over the bed and put my left leg down first. The next thing I knew I was sprawling on the floor, and it took a few nurses to get me back into the bed. I still wasn't having the bed pan treatment, though, and trust me, I soon learned how to walk over to the toilet when I needed to go.

I spent 10 nights in hospital and was visited by the club doctor and the surgeon at regular intervals. The diagnosis wasn't good, as my ligaments had been ripped from the bone and I had to have surgery to repair the whole knee. I was gutted. Not only was my season over and I was running the risk of being permanently replaced at centre back, but it would take at least another six months for me to actually get back on the field. To say that I was heartbroken and deflated is an understatement to say the least, but the feeling didn't last long, as I was soon back at the club and in the gym working on my calves and thighs in order to build them back up. If I hadn't done that, I would have risked the muscles just wasting away. There was no way that this was going to happen. It was going to be a long road back, but I was determined to get there. I had to!

Harry Redknapp had been incensed by the tackle made by Paul Moulden in that fateful practice match – so much so that he sold the striker just a few weeks later. I never held it against Moulden, though, as it was never intentional in my eyes, and I hold no grudge against him about it.

During my time in hospital and in the gym, I didn't have any contact with Harry Redknapp. That didn't bother me too much, as it was standard practice with him, but an incident with Carol at Dean Court left me fuming and ended up with me in Harry's office.

All the players at the club had their own areas in the offices that were used typically for fan mail, amongst other things. With the injury that I had just sustained, I hadn't been able to collect mine, so Carol had agreed to go and pick up my things on my behalf. I was happy for her to do that, as I guess I needed cheering up a little. At that time, Carol wasn't driving, so our good friend Tony Brown gave her a lift to the club.

Carol tells the story better than I do: "I got into Tony's car and off we went to Dean Court to pick up the mail. Tony stayed in the car and waited for me. I went into the offices and had a chat with the office staff. It was all nice and cordial. They were asking how Shaun was and requested that I give him their best and tell him they were thinking of him. I told them I would do that, picked up all the post and said my goodbyes. I went back to the car park and walked to Tony's car when I heard someone behind me shouting all kinds of profanities. At first, I didn't think it was aimed at me, but when I looked around, I saw that Harry Redknapp was looking straight at me. He continued to use vile language. It sounded like he was saying something about me 'ruling the roost over Shaun' and 'he should be back in the club by now'.

"I couldn't believe what I was hearing. It shook me badly. I got into Tony's car and I burst into tears. Tony had heard everything that had taken place and couldn't believe what he'd heard either. We drove home, and I couldn't hide how upset I was when I saw Shaun."

I was so angry when Carol told me what had taken place. It was totally uncalled for and none of it made any sense. I wasn't going to take all this sitting down, so I comforted Carol and asked Tony to take me to the club straight away. When I got there, I'd like to say that I stormed in, but that would have been difficult with my injury. I had it out with Harry and told him that he had been out of order and demanded an apology, which was forthcoming, but I am not sure it was heartfelt. I then went back to Carol, relayed what had taken place and then we just got on with it. It was never mentioned again by us or in the presence of Harry.

So imagine our surprise some years later when Harry recalled the incident in a book that he had written called *Always Managing: My Autobiography*. In the book, he said, "At Bournemouth, Shaun Teale's missus nearly ran me over after a row over about one hundred quid. She marched down to the training ground over some minor contractual issue and gave me a mouthful. The next thing I knew she was reversing out of the car park so fast she nearly took me with her."

When we were made aware of what had been written, we were totally flabbergasted. None of it was true. I had been happy with the £50 increases Harry had given me. I only wanted to read my fan mail, and more importantly, Carol wasn't even able to drive, so how could she have tried to run Harry over? At least we are now able to set the record straight with my side of the story.

Other people have taken issue with Harry's book as well, including Julian Dicks. He denied Harry's account of him once turning up two days late to the start of pre-season training, and Steven Gerrard refuted a claim in the book that he texted Redknapp a message of support in the days leading up to Roy Hodgson's appointment as England manager.

Interesting stuff!

I spent some time at Lilleshall with the FA working on my

fitness. I can tell you it was like purgatory for me! The routine was more like training for the SAS than for football. I was put into a swimming pool and told just to keep on treading water. It went on for so long that I was having trouble keeping my head above water. I had just had major knee surgery and I was put on machines where I would have to undertake loads of leg curls that hurt like hell. If I didn't finish the number that I had to do, I would have to start again. The physios all stood around me with their clipboards, nodding away to each other. It was at that moment that I fully understood how that character Private Pyle in the film *Full Metal Jacket* goes mad and shoots his sergeant to death!

That training lasted for a week and then I was back to Bournemouth working with the physios on a daily basis. I was just in time to witness our fall into the Second Division. It was just awful, and I was powerless to do anything about it other than offer my support in the dressing room and around the training ground. Mentally I was kicking or heading balls out every time our opponents were attacking us at every game I went to, but in reality, that was all I could do. I hated every moment of it.

We had come to the last game of the season and we were at home to Leeds United. It seemed that the whole of Leeds had come down to Bournemouth to see their team crowned champions. For us, though, it was the total opposite, as we were relegated and heading back to the Third Division. The disparity could not have been bigger. Despite the fact I had missed the last dozen games, I still managed to bag the Player of the Season award, and I was presented with the trophy on the pitch, and with my crutches, just before kick-off. From a personal point of view, it was great to receive the award, but it felt hollow in many ways due to our total capitulation and subsequent relegation.

I very nearly didn't make it onto the pitch that day and could easily have accepted my award wearing a brick in my head, because a certain faction of the Leeds supporters had decided to mix celebrations with rioting at the stadium and around the town. We had been warned this might happen, and I had told Carol to stop at home with the kids, as it was probably not going to be safe for them. I went with a friend who drove me to the stadium. Throughout that journey we could hear the police sirens and see the helicopters in the air, so we knew that keeping our families at home was the right thing to do. We got to the ground (eventually) and made our way into the stadium, carefully avoiding the bricks being thrown at us by the away fans. It was a boiling hot day as well, and it must have sapped the Leeds fans' energy picking up and throwing the bricks as many times as they did! Leeds won the game 1-0, and the townsfolk must have been relieved in Bournemouth in the following days knowing that the two teams would be separated in the league for the following season, at least unless there were cup draws on the south coast.

My first full season as a professional footballer had ended badly for me, as well as for the team in general, despite the accolades and awards I'd gained. I had also won the Mickey Cave Supporters Player of the Year award. Mickey had been a fan favourite during the early part of the 1970s, and it was a real honour to get the award.

There was another incident with Harry in the summer of 1990 that ended in absolute tragedy, and it happened during the World Cup finals in Italy. Harry was travelling to and from matches in the company of Michael Sinclair, who was the chairman of York City, Fred Whitehouse of Aston Villa, and Bournemouth's managing director, Brian Tiler. Their chauffeur-driven minibus was involved in a head-on collision with a car containing three Italian soldiers. The collision was so bad that the minibus was flipped onto its roof and skidded 50 yards along the road. Brian Tiler and the three soldiers were killed straight away. Harry was doused in petrol but was pulled clear by Sinclair. Harry also suffered a fractured skull, a broken nose, cracked ribs and a gash in his left leg. He had been very lucky, as had the other passengers who had survived this awful incident.

It was a solemn occasion as we returned for pre-season training for obvious reasons. We all sat down and spoke about Brian Tiler, sharing stories, and we attended the memorial for him. Harry himself was not able to continue with his job in the capacity that he was used to, and Tony Pulis and Terry Shanahan ran training alongside Stuart Morgan, so the focus on football-related matters continued unabated. Eventually Harry came back into the reckoning full time, and whilst we never forgot about Brian, we got back down to the business in hand. For me, this was to get back playing and help the team get back its Second Division status as quickly as possible.

Bournemouth were one of the favourites for promotion in the 1990–1991 season, but that didn't quite turn out as planned. We finished in ninth position at the end of the season, although we were just three points behind the team that finished seventh, Bury, the occupiers of the last playoff spot. We had taken four points off them as well during the campaign, drawing 1-1 at home and winning 4-2 away. It was our away form that let us down, with only five wins, seven draws and eleven defeats on the road. Contrast that with our home form, which saw us pick up fourteen home wins, seven draws and only three defeats.

We were prolific at home, and our winning margins were mainly by a goal or two. However, there were times when we played away from Dean Court and got thrashed. These included a 5-0 defeat at Grimsby Town, a 4-1 at Bolton Wanderers and a 4-0 at Cambridge United. Two of these teams went up automatically (Grimsby and Cambridge) and Bolton made the playoffs, so at least we lost to teams that were better placed than us. At the end of the season, our goal difference was basically playing off scratch in golf terms. We'd scored 58 over the season and shipped the same amount. Millwall knocked us out of the League Cup in the second round, and we managed to get through to the fourth round of the FA Cup before being spanked at Newcastle United 5-1. Remember that when we lost away games in 1990–1991, we lost big time!

For the second season on the trot, I won the Player of the Year award, and I managed to get a full season under my belt as well. This meant a lot to me after the major injury I had suffered the year before. I really enjoyed the season overall, although I was the cause of Harry Redknapp losing £100 in a bet with Stuart Morgan.

I came down with a rather nasty bout of chickenpox, but luckily there had been a break in games, so I was able to plan a good recovery for myself. I let the club know that I wouldn't be in for a few days and basically stayed away from people. I'd had chickenpox as a kid but never as bad as I had it as an adult. I had spots on top of spots and in all kinds of funny places! Either

Harry had forgotten I'd had it or the memo hadn't reached his desk. Either way, he was perplexed when I wasn't at training. According to Stuart, this is how the conversation went:

Harry: Where's Tealey?
Stuart: He's got chickenpox.
Harry: Farkin' 'ell. No one told me. We bleedin' need him!
Stuart: I'll call him.
Harry: Nah, don't bother if he's got the pox.
Stuart: But you know what Tealey is like. He will come in regardless if he's needed.
Harry: £100 says he won't.
Stuart: You're on, Harry.
Both men shook hands.

I then got the call from Stuart. He made no mention of the bet and asked if I would come in. As it happened, the pox had started to clear up well. I still had the spots, but it wasn't contagious. So as soon as I put the phone down, I made my way to Dean Court. I told the lads that it wasn't contagious, but they still didn't come near me. I was waiting for a specific word to be used to describe what I looked like, but it wasn't forthcoming until Harry clapped eyes on me. The place had gone quiet for a second or two as everybody waited with bated breath for what Harry would say. "Farkin' 'ell, Tealey," he bellowed, "you look like a farkin' leper. All you need is the cloak."

Harry was deadly serious, but the rest of us just fell about laughing. I didn't put a cloak on but was really glad to wear my training top – a professional training top at that. I never allowed myself to forget my roots in non-league football and the rejections I had experienced along the way. I was still very grateful for where I had got to and was looking forward to another season in the Third Division battling it out for Bournemouth and getting them back up to the second tier and maybe beyond. Notts County had made it to the First Division, so there was no reason why we couldn't, although that seemed to be a few years off at the very least. I would have to bide my time and play to the best of my ability and see whether the promised land of playing in England's top flight was a reality or just a pipe dream. As it happened, my last game for Bournemouth was on 11 May 1991 and it was a 3-1 loss at Gay Meadow, which was the home of Shrewsbury Town. We finished ninth in Division Three.

Little did I know just how close I actually was to the top flight. I was soon to swap playing home games on the coast for somewhere slap bang in the middle of the country. I would have no sea to look out on, but I would be able to call myself a First Division footballer.

Fair trade, I think.

CHAPTER EIGHT
Aston Villa

THE ASTON VILLA move had come totally out of the blue. Carol, the kids and I had been on holiday in Lanzarote. It was the first proper holiday we'd had together, just the four of us, and we had a brilliant time. The only issue that we had was our plane broke down in Lanzarote and we weren't able to fly back until the following day. It was Friday and I was due to return for pre-season training with Bournemouth the following day. I didn't want to be making waves before the season had started. I phoned the offices at Bournemouth and was told that it would not be an issue, that Harry would be expecting me on the Monday for pre-season training instead. At least I had sorted that part out. We were put up in a local hotel and then flew back on the Saturday.

I don't know exactly what happened in between calling Bournemouth on the Friday to let them know our situation and walking through the door with our suitcases the next day, but it was life changing for me and my family. Carol's mum and dad were stopping in our house so we didn't have to worry about it whilst we were away. They had popped out, and whilst they had done so, Harry Redknapp had called and left a message for us. It was to tell me to get in touch with him as soon as possible, which I did the minute I got in. "Leave the unpacking to Carol," were Harry's first words. "You are going to meet Ron Atkinson, and if all goes well, he is going to sign you for Aston Villa." I was a little dumbstruck to say the least. My mind went blank for a few seconds. *Where do Aston Villa play and what league are they in?* were my first thoughts.

My heart was racing. *Play your cards right, Shaun, and soon you'll be a First Division player.* I tried to remain as calm as

I could when I told Carol that I needed to pop into town and meet with Villa's manager. I recall that Carol just looked at me and nodded, as if to say *go and meet Ron*. She knew what it would mean, and as always, she gave me her full support.

I met Ron Atkinson at the Royal Bath Hotel in Bournemouth, not far from the sea front. He was sitting in a corner, trying to be inconspicuous, but it never really worked – it wasn't Ron's style, was it? I half expected the local media to be sitting there with him, but luckily there was no one around. If there had been, they would have been privy to one of the weirdest questions that has even been posed to me as a footballer about to be transferred.

We shook hands, introduced ourselves and sat down to talk. Then came Ron's opening gambit: "What are your strengths, Shaun?"

At first, I just looked at him and couldn't figure out what to say. *Is he asking me seriously or is he joking?* The look on his face informed me that it was the former! *If he wants to buy me, then surely he knows what he's purchasing already and what I could bring to his new team?*

"Well," I replied, "I am a team player first and foremost and will always put the team first. It's important to me that I develop a great relationship with my central defence partner and those on the left-hand side of me, as well as the rest of the defence, midfield and attack. I'm also strong in the air." It felt really strange for me to have to say all this, because I naturally thought that Ron would know this already.

Ron just sat there and didn't say a word at first. I think he was sounding me out, trying to see if I was on the level. I was with him for just over an hour. During that time, Ron did all the talking, setting out his vision for the club and what he wanted to achieve. He also outlined what the deal would be, and then he asked me one other question, which was equally baffling. "Shaun, one last question. What car do you drive?"

Again, I just sat there wondering if this was some kind of joke, but yet again he had a poker face.

I had a Ford Orion at the time and I told him so. He told me that I could not come to Villa in that car, and as there were no club cars available, he would give me £15,000 to buy a new one. So I bought my first Mercedes, which cost me £11,000, plus I got

£4,000 for mine in part exchange. So I eventually banked £8,000 on the deal!

Unfortunately, the Merc didn't last long, as I managed to blow the engine up one day on my way back from the training ground. I replaced it with a brand new Mercedes.

I later received my first ever official club car, a Rover 416 GSI automatic. While it wasn't as flash as my Merc, the fact I'd been given a car reminded me of just how far I had come in my career.

Anyway, at the end of the meeting, Ron nodded, shook my hand and told me to start packing my bags, as I would be an Aston Villa player within the next few days. He obviously liked my strengths – even though he didn't like my car!

After we shook hands, I informed Ron that I'd get back to him as soon as I had spoken to Carol, and then I drove home in a daze. I was 27 and I was about to sign for one of the biggest clubs in the country and play for one of the top managers. All my dreams were coming true.

Just a few days earlier, we were packing to come home from a lovely holiday, thinking about pre-season training with Bournemouth and the prospect of a season in the third tier. It's strange how things change so quickly in professional sport. I got home and told Carol about the Villa deal and the opportunity. I would receive a £50,000 signing-on fee and £1,500-per-week, while Bournemouth would be receiving £350,000 as a transfer fee. It didn't take long for Carol to agree to this. We were hitting the big time, and our hard work was finally paying off. It was sad to leave Bournemouth after nearly three seasons, but this was the kind of opportunity that only came around once, and I just couldn't afford to pass it up.

Very soon, I found that I was travelling up to the Midlands. I travelled up alone by train, as Carol wanted to sort out some things in Bournemouth. I was met by Ron Atkinson and his driver at Birmingham International railway station. I couldn't miss his car in the car park – a British racing green Rolls Royce. Ron had picked up the nickname of Mr Bojangles, and I instantly knew why he had acquired it. I was driven to the Arden Hotel, which was situated very close to the station, and dropped off there. Ron advised me to take it easy that night, as I would be picked up the following day and taken for training and then I'd be off for Villa's pre-season tour of Germany soon afterwards. It was a good job I had brought my passport with me! I had a quiet meal; after I spoke to Carol on the phone, I went to bed. I didn't really get that much sleep, though, as I was too excited thinking about what was ahead for me and my new team in the top flight.

Aston Villa's training ground was at Bodymoor Heath, North Warwickshire, just a few miles from the hotel I was staying in. I had heard so many good things about the facilities there; it was one of the premier training grounds in the country. I couldn't wait to see it for myself, but when I was picked up the next morning, I was told that training was taking place in Bournville, which was on the other side of Birmingham! Bodymoor Heath was having some work done on it. What I didn't realise was that the substitute training ground was at Cadbury, the home of the world-famous chocolate company. I made a mental note that we would visit the factory where the chocolate was made when Carol and the boys came up to live with me. It may not have been Willy Wonka's chocolate factory, and I was certainly no Charlie, but I really felt that I had been given the Golden Ticket to top-flight football in the country.

I must admit that I was a little nervous when that training session at Cadbury got underway. I had never felt this way before on my first day with any of my previous clubs, but I guess this was down to the fact that I was now playing in the top division. When I talk to Villa fans nowadays, I'm always told that when I signed for the club, I was a total unknown, and it was the same for the players. Most didn't have a clue who I was!

I needn't have worried about it, though, as the players and the fans welcomed me with open arms. The first thing I noticed was that the intensity of the actual training was far greater than it had been in the lower leagues. I knew I would have to work harder than I had ever done before.

The first players that I got to know during that session were my fellow centre halves, Paul McGrath, Derek Mountfield and Kent Nielsen. It was obvious by the sheer size of the squad that some players had come in and others wanted to leave.

The only player I knew was Kevin Richardson, who had only recently joined the club himself. I knew him from my Everton days, and it was good to see a friendly face. He'd had a good career with Watford and Arsenal and in Spain for Real Sociedad. That first session finished and after getting changed, we were taken to Birmingham Airport, where we flew out to Germany for the pre-season tour. I had never been on a pre-season tour before, so I found it really exciting.

We flew to Düsseldorf before being driven to Hanover. I remember the coach went up a really large and steep mountain; it was so steep, I thought we were going to need oxygen masks! When we reached the top, we were presented with the sight of one of the most beautiful hotels I have ever seen. It was so high up, there was no one around us. We could work hard and play hard without really being troubled. It had been a long journey from Birmingham, and the worst part for me was that I hadn't been able to engage in one of my favourite pastimes – smoking. Yes, smoking.

I had managed to steal moments away in the toilets at Birmingham and Düsseldorf Airports, chewing as much gum as I could to hide the smell. I was new to the team, and on the coach going up that mountain, I started to wonder who I would be sharing a room with. I was really hoping that it would be a fellow dragster or, at the very least, not a grass or teacher's pet!

We were in the foyer of the hotel when Jim Barron, who was Ron's assistant, shouted over, "Tealey, you're sharing with Les."

The person in question was Les Sealey, the Villa goalkeeper. He had also played for Manchester United and Luton Town, so I knew who he was, but I doubt if he knew who I was. I had heard that he was one of those confident Cockney types who was certainly not afraid to hear his own voice and provide his opinion.

As we walked to our room, Les didn't say a word to me. *Have I upset him or doesn't he like me?* I had absolutely no idea either way, but we became good mates as soon as the door was shut. Les put down his bags and did no more than take out a cigar, light it and bellow, "Thank fuck for that. I've been wanting this for a couple of hours now."

I almost said the same thing but just smiled at him as I lit up my cigarette. Les Sealey certainly wasn't a teacher's pet! From that moment on, we got on very well. I was a northerner and he was a southerner, and neither of us were wallflowers, that's for sure! The rest of the lads christened our dorm 'The Tealey and the Sealey room'!

On that first night, we all had dinner and I got to know the lads better. They all made me feel very welcome. The next morning was our first training session. I was about a week or so behind the lads in terms of sharpness, as they had been together getting fit while I'd been in Lanzarote. It was a hard session, and I could certainly feel it, but I was determined to work that bit harder to catch up, and I stayed behind to do some extra training. This continued for the following day. Ron wasn't there for day two, though, as he was travelling to Italy with David Platt to tie up his world record move of £5.5 million from Villa to Bari.

Platty had experienced a great Italia '90 and had continued his rich form for the club during the 1990–1991 season, but he had made no secret of the fact that he wanted the move. I was gutted that I only got to work with him for one day. While Ron was away, Jim Barron and the ex-Villa striker Andy Gray took training. We were basically given a couple of hours off, and Les suggested that we walk into the town, which was about a mile away. So off we went for a coffee and a good old smoke.

It had been a very steep drive to get to the hotel, and whilst it was great walking down, we decided that it might be a good idea to get a taxi back. The place was just beautiful. It had cafes and designer stores. We soon found a little bar and headed into it. It was at this stage that I first came across Paul McGrath and learned of his issues with drinking. Paul was sitting in the corner, and he looked totally pissed. This shocked me a little, but Les just tutted and raised his eyebrows as if this was nothing new. I had heard the rumours and read in the papers that Paul was a big drinker, and apparently this was the reason why Alex Ferguson moved him (and others) on. He was sitting down behind a large round table that was full of bottles of beer. The barman informed us that he had come in on his own and that the empties were all his. We did no more than order that taxi and take Paul back to the hotel. When we arrived, we knocked on Jim Walker's door. Jim had played football when he was younger but had trained to be a physiotherapist, and this was the role he had taken up at Villa. We had put Paul in the best hands. Jim knew all about Paul's issues, and he thanked us for bringing him back and said he would deal with it from there. By that time, we hadn't even managed to get that coffee, but we had looked after Paul, and that was far more important. We were due back to training in the afternoon, so we didn't venture back out again. When we got back to training, we were told that we would be playing head tennis exercises on the concrete tennis courts. I was up for that, and all the lads put on trainers instead of football boots.

The last person I thought I would see back for the afternoon session was Paul McGrath, but there he was making his way down to the tennis courts. I now understood why Jim Walker was the go-to man for him. He had worked wonders considering how pissed Paul had been. The issue was that Paul turned up in his football boots and not his trainers. Andy Gray had told him that he didn't have time to go back and change. During the session it was like watching Bambi on Ice as he fell all over the place; he was slipping and sliding and just falling all over the place! The players weren't laughing, though, as they knew what he was like and how the drink affected him. He was one of the team and therefore we had his back. I had helped him myself a couple of hours earlier, and it would not be the last time, either. Andy Gray had seen enough and instructed Jim to take Paul back to his room and basically lock him in.

We carried on with our training session and then afterwards we made our way back to the hotel. However, we spotted Paul sat in the bar ordering drink after drink. Jim had taken Paul's money off him and locked him in his room, but Paul had still managed to get out. He had gone down to the bar and ordered drinks and requested that they be put on the club's tab. We found out later that his escape route was shimmying down the drainpipe!

So, whilst Paul was a heavy drinker, I was a smoker. It never really got me into trouble, except once at Bournemouth when we played a pre-season match at Tottenham. We got thrashed, and this upset Harry Redknapp. He tore into me afterwards and told me in no uncertain terms that I would have played better if I wasn't smoking tabs.

Villa played three games in Germany but I didn't get onto the pitch in any of them. I was OK with that, as I was basically using the time to address my fitness and observe life with First Division footballers.

My first actual appearance in Villa colours came in a pre-season friendly at Villa Park against Wolverhampton Wanderers on a Friday night. It was part of Paul Birch's testimonial celebrations. David Platt came onto the pitch to kick the game off in his Bari kit, the team he had signed for in Italy a few days previously. It was all a bit strange, but it was a good way for Platty to sign off his Villa career and applaud the fans. Ron Atkinson was able to rebuild his squad with a good percentage of the Platt fee, so it was a good deal all round. Whilst some of us had arrived before the England international had moved to Bari, perhaps the club knew that it was going to happen and therefore sanctioned the arrival of me, Kevin Richardson, Paul Mortimer, Les Sealey, Steve Staunton, Ugo Ehiogu, Dalian Atkinson and the legend that was Cyrille Regis.

Now I'd had my first appearance in the famous claret and blue, I couldn't wait for the 1991–1992 season to begin. While Carol was concluding business in Bournemouth, Villa put me up in the Trust House Forte hotel in Great Barr, not far from Junction 7 of the M6, although far enough that I couldn't hear the traffic. The added bonus was that it was only a couple of miles away from Villa Park, with Bodymoor Heath just a few miles further.

Also staying at the hotel were Kevin Richardson, Paul Mortimer and Steve Staunton, so we car shared to training.

My first team debut came on Saturday 17 August 1991. It was a real baptism of fire, not just for me but for the rest of the debutants who ran out onto the Hillsborough pitch to face newly promoted Sheffield Wednesday on a boiling hot day. Moreover, for Ron Atkinson, because he had been in charge of Wednesday during the previous season.

Ron had done very well at Wednesday, achieving promotion and winning the League Cup with them, but the Wednesday fans didn't like the fact that he had left them to join us, and there was a lot of animosity in the air. Before his spell with the Owls, he had also managed West Bromwich Albion (twice) and Manchester United, where he had won two FA Cups with the Red Devils.

Ron was born in Liverpool but moved to Birmingham as a

child, and it was well known in football circles that he had a soft spot for Aston Villa. He had even been on their books as a player before forging a career at Oxford United. Villa chairman Doug Ellis had tried to lure Big Ron to the club as soon as the 1990–1991 season had finished, although he had initially turned Villa down. Amazingly, just a week or so later he did a U-turn and became Aston Villa's new boss, to the absolute sheer delight of the Villa faithful.

However, it's fair to say that the Wednesday fans saw it completely the other way. They were disappointed and, more to the point, very angry. So when the fixtures came out and pitted us away at Hillsborough on the opening day of the season, the media lapped it up and fuelled the flames even more. In a weird kind of way, it made it easier for the players, especially us new ones, to be able to concentrate on ourselves, as all the attention was on Ron.

We arrived at the ground a couple of hours before kick-off; you could feel the tension in the air and cut it with a knife. I have never seen so many police officers waiting for the coach to turn up before a game. All sorts of missiles were thrown at the team bus. All you could hear as we got off the coach was "Judas" repeated over and over by angry voices. We knew that Ron had felt nervous on the bus, but he didn't show it when he walked down the steps. In fact, he was smiling – or was it grimacing? We were all relieved to get into the sanctity of the dressing room. We were told to get out and shut the Wednesday fans up as quickly as possible.

It didn't quite turn out that way, though, because Wednesday took the lead after just three minutes through David Hirst, and then, after 36 minutes, we found ourselves 2-0 down. Three-quarters of the 36,000 in the ground erupted. At the time it was by far the biggest crowd that I had played in front of.

"Judas, Judas, what's the score?" reverberated around the famous old stadium.

It was looking bad for us, but we managed to pull a goal back through Cyrille Regis, right in front of the Villa fans in the Leppings Lane end. This was the first time that the Leppings Lane end had been open since the tragic Hillsborough disaster just two years earlier.

By the time the half-time whistle blew, we were back in the game, and all we wanted to do was get straight back out there. It only took us a couple of minutes after the break to level the match and, ironically, it was Dalian Atkinson who put the ball into the back of the net.

Ron wasn't the only Atkinson coming back to Sheffield Wednesday that day. Dalian had also played for them. Welcome home, boys!

And then we sealed the victory with just five minutes to go when a third debutant scored, Steve Staunton.

So many debuts, so much hate, and in the end, we turned likely defeat into a stunning victory. The dressing room was buzzing after the match, and you can imagine the smile on Ron's face. It's fair to say that we got changed as quickly as we could and boarded the coach to get away from the stadium.

I was pleased with my overall game, and even more so with our recovery and second-half performance. One game played, one win. We were up and running.

We had six players making their debuts. The starting 11 that played for Villa that day were:

Goalkeeper: Nigel Spink.
Defence: Paul McGrath, Steve Staunton, Shaun Teale, Derek Mountfield.
Midfield: Gordon Cowans, Paul Mortimer, Kevin Richardson.
Attack: Dalian Atkinson, Cyrille Regis, Dwight Yorke.

I really started to feel part of the team from early on at Villa, and that victory was just the icing on the cake. To make things even better was the arrival of Carol and the boys. We moved into a house on Sir Alfred's Way, Walmley in Sutton Coldfield, a leafy suburb situated to the north of Birmingham. It was a popular place with Villa players while I played for the club, and it still is. When we first moved in, Kent Nielsen and Ivo Stas lived in the area too. It was great for borrowing sugar!

Just round the corner from us was Dwight Yorke, although he would eventually end up buying our house, which meant we saw our old bedrooms splashed all over the Sunday tabloids, but more of that little story later.

I had a great time at Weymouth. I knew that moving down south would get me my dream move into professional football.

I was proud to represent my country in a non-league capacity.

TEALE

Debut boy makes it all look easy

BIRMINGHAM CITY...... 0
AFC BOURNEMOUTH ... 1

PETER ROBINSON AT ST ANDREWS

Shaun Teale passed his first full test in the Football League with flying colours - and immediately prepared to be axed for AFC Bournemouth's FA Cup showdown with Manchester United.

The 24-year-old discovery from non-league Weymouth made a stunning first full appearance for the Cherries at St Andrews.

But his break into the football big time is guaranteed to be short-lived.

going to be much better people than that I'm going to have to deal with in the future."

Bournemouth didn't make the most impressive of starts, however.

Indeed, in the first half, with the wind against them, they did precious little.

The only bright spots in a paralysingly dull 45 minutes were the wing play of Birmingham's best player, Steve Wigley, and a volley that flew high and wide from Steve Whitton.

After the interval, and after a Redknapp rocket in the dressing room, matters improved.

Luther Blissett was brought down seconds after AFC kicked off, and Ian Bishop, another outstanding figure for the Cherries, stepped up to take the free kick.

I got the man of the match award on my full debut for Bournemouth. Carol and I bought all the newspapers after this game!

WEEKEND CHERRIES with Derek McGregor

The two faces of Shaun

There's a quiet side

CHERRIES unflinching defender Shaun Teale takes no prisoners on the pitch — but he still thinks he is a soft touch.

Fierce competitiveness is such an important part of this 26-year-old's game.

But get his boys Nathan and Ryan around him and it is hard to believe this is the player who mid-week tamed 6ft 3in Tranmere Rovers colossus Jim Steel who weighs in at 14 stone.

"I've got two faces, " revealed Teale. "At home I'm quiet and I play with the kids. But once I get my kit on my personality totally changes. I don't like being a loser — and I never intend to be in life.

"As a person I've never had a problem with determination but I can be very easy going — too much so at times."

Teale is no kicker or assassin but life in non-League football with Southport, Northwich Victoria and Weymouth taught him to look after himself. His uncompromising style, coupled with superb aerial strength and pace make him an impressive defender.

The absence of those crucial qualities cost Cherries dearly in the last two months of the 1989-90 season. Relegation was more agony for Teale as he recovered from a medial ligament operation.

"It was flattering to hear people say my absence cost the lads their place in the Second Division, " he said. "But one player does not make a team.

"It was the worst injury of my career. The pain wasn't too bad, the worst part was the time factor. It just dragged on so long."

Teale's distribution is the weakest part of his game and he knows it. "I made 25 passes at Preston, " he said. "I've never did that before. Over half found their man so I must be getting better."

A proud Northerner and patter merchant, Teale has a close bond with Cherries supporters.

"I'm like Sean O'Driscoll. Win lose or draw I will always go into the supporters club for a drink, " he explained. "At the end of the day they pay our wages."

The respect is mutual. Teale was a clear winner at the end of the season when votes were counted for the Mickey Cave Supporters Player of the Year award.

"I will never forget the Leeds United game when I received the award on the pitch, " said Teale. "That was my biggest moment in football."

Teale's best mate in football is Wolves striker Andy Mutch. "I've known him since I was six, " he said.

Oldham's Andy Ritchie rates as Teale's toughest opponent. "I've not met anyone harder than Andy, " he revealed.

"Andy gave me my toughest afternoon in league football."

Teale also has fond memories of the day several years ago when he marked a certain Andy Jones out of a match.

"He was playing for Rhyl and I was with Southport in the Northern Premier League. I marked him and we won 5-0.

"It was nice to remind him when he signed last week, " chuckled Teale.

Shaun Teale factfile

Birthplace: Southport **Date of birth:** March 10, 1964.

Biggest influence on career: Stuart Morgan. He plucked me out of nowhere and got me to Weymouth. At the time I was with Northwich Victoria and it was not easy trying to persuade players to leave that far from the North. The rest is history.

Worst part of life as a footballer: Being away from my family.

Funniest person at Dean Court: Peter Guthrie — he's a headbanger! I've known since my Weymouth days and he really is a lunatic. He loves taking the mickey.

Cherries player I most admire: Sean O'Driscoll. His work rate is phenomenal and he never gives anything less than 110 per cent. He would admit he is not the most skilful of players but he is all heart.

Ambition: To play in the First Division. **Contract:** June 1994.

Ideal night out: A quiet drink with wife Carol.

FAMILY MAN— Shaun Teale

I love this piece written by my good mate Derek McGregor.

Home sweet home with the boys and Carol.

Posing with the new car and the fam!

A whole new ball game – Villa's first ever game in the Premiership in 1992.

The famous yellow kit that Villa wore once against Liverpool in the FA Cup.

With my wonderful Carol.
I love her more each day.

On the radio with Tom Ross from BRMB in Birmingham.

Tealey's up for the ball.

Doing the hokey cokey with Chelsea's Tony Cascarino .

I look like I am about to do a Tommy Cooper impression!

Oh sit down! My famous smile after getting Villa back in the tie in the League Cup semi final against Tranmere in 1994.

Having a good chat with Bryan Robson before the League Cup final in 1994.

We made it Carol! With the League Cup.

Signalling to an opponent that he better stop or I am going to put him on his arse.

With the Villa fans. I've always had a great rapport with them and still do to this day.

I really enjoyed my four seasons with Aston Villa.

Despite a busy summer, Big Ron wasn't finished with his transfer business. Out went established players such as Chris Price, Nigel Callaghan and, eventually, Kent and Ivo.

The feel-good factor wasn't just confined to the dressing room after the win at Sheffield Wednesday – it was felt on the terraces too. The first league game of the season at Villa Park drew almost 40,000 fans. I couldn't believe the atmosphere when I ran out for the mid-week game against Manchester United. I had goosebumps on my goosebumps!

We lost the game 1-0 through a Steve Bruce penalty. Bryan Robson won the spot kick after he was adjudged to have been fouled by Gordon Cowans, nicknamed Sid. The TV commentator made a point of the fact that I walked away in disgust. I certainly did, as there was no way it should have been a penalty.

I had partnered Derek Mountfield in defence for both the United and Wednesday matches, but that was the last game Derek played for the Villa, as he was transferred to Wolves soon after. Making way for Derek was Ugo Ehiogu. He slotted in well, and I could tell he was going to be a good player for us.

Winning a game and then losing one set the tone in the first month or so of the season. We beat Arsenal 3-1 at Villa Park just a few days later. We played so well that day, and it was no mean feat, as Arsenal were the current champions. One of our goal scorers was Gary Penrice. He had the nickname of Piss Pot. It wasn't that he was a drinker or had no money or even a weak bladder, it just went with Penrice! I got on well with Gary, but he was never really in Ron's long-term plans, so we knew he would be off soon.

We then lost by the same score at West Ham United. After that defeat, we only picked up two points from the next five games, but we were back to winning ways against Nottingham Forest on 21 September. It was a significant match for me, as I got my name on the score sheet after just 12 seconds, although unfortunately it was an own goal. Forest went on the attack straight after kick-off. The ball went over Stan – Steve Staunton – and I was covering him. I tried to play the ball back to Nigel Spink, but I lobbed it high and too hard, and it went over Spinksy into the net. I couldn't believe it. As a central defender, it's par for the course that you'll score a few own goals, but they are normally deflections that you can do nothing about. This was more like the kind of goal a striker would score when he saw the goalkeeper off his line! I felt gutted and embarrassed all at the same time. The lads consoled me, and I dusted myself down. Luckily we got our act together in the second half and won 3-1 to spare my blushes somewhat!

As usual, we followed up a win with a defeat before we went on our best run of the season, winning five games on the trot to move ourselves right up the table. Then we had our best win of the season, beating Luton Town 4-0 at Villa Park. We only conceded one goal during that time, so we were pretty pleased with ourselves in the defensive department.

At the end of November, we came up against Leeds United, and the game was broadcast live on ITV. The problem was that Leeds were flying, and they continued their excellent run, beating us 4-1 at Villa Park. Leeds were just too good for us on the day, and Rod Wallace and Lee Chapman ran us ragged. The weather was just awful, but we couldn't use it as an excuse. The game was notable, as it was the last game that Gordon Cowans played for the Villa. Sid was a legend, having won the League Championship, European Cup and League Cup during the first of three spells at Villa Park. He was a beautiful footballer and one of the best number tens in the game. He was and still is a great bloke as well.

My partnership with Paul McGrath in the centre of defence was blossoming. Macca had started the season as a right back but moved back into the centre when Derek Mountfield left. Ron had brought in another right back called Dariusz Kubicki, from Poland. We also brought in Garry Parker from Nottingham Forest late in 1991 as the squad and team took shape. The only issue of note had been Paul Mortimer, who only lasted a couple of months at the club. I don't think he settled too well in the Midlands and away from London, and it came as no surprise when he returned to Charlton.

We saw out the remaining five games of 1991 with three wins and two defeats, so overall it had been a respectable return considering just how many new players had come and gone.

During that winter, Ron called me and Kevin Richardson into

his office. There was an international break coming up, and as we had played in every game, he told us to have a week off to get some sun and relax. That news really pleased me – not so much the idea of getting away, but the fact that I had only been a top-flight player for a few months and was being recognised for it. We managed to get out to Cyprus, and Rico ended up in Portugal with his family. We thought it was a lovely touch from Ron.

The second half of the season didn't bode as well as the first, as we only won six more games, scoring just four league goals from the start of January 1992 until the end of March. During that period, we went five games without scoring as well. There were not many plus points, although we did get a goalless draw at Leeds, who went on to become champions. Both games against the champions-elect saw some atrocious weather conditions. At home we had gales, and away it was the snow that affected the game, but it seemed to suit us more than it did them, in fairness. Carol had come up for the game with the club shop manager, John Greenfield, and I was surprised they made it there. I remember looking up at her in the stands and she looked frozen.

We managed to score eleven goals in the last six matches, with four wins and two defeats. We had our biggest away win of the season during that period when we beat Spurs 5-2. I scored my second own goal of the season, but again the team won, so it turned out OK. I didn't try to lob the keeper this time, though! What made that win even better was that my own goal had made it 2-0 to Spurs, but we fought back to earn an emphatic victory.

We finished the season with a 2-0 home victory against Coventry City, with Big Cyrille bagging one just like he had done in the very first game against Sheffield Wednesday.

Overall, we finished seventh in the league, four points behind Liverpool and ten behind Manchester City. Who knows what might have happened if we hadn't gone on that bad run at the start of 1992? But given how many players had come and gone during this transitional period, it was a decent season.

The cup competitions were a disappointment, although I did manage to score my first goal for Villa against Grimsby Town in the second round of the League Cup. It was a diving header in the 70th minute. However, it wasn't good enough to take us through, as Grimsby won the two legs via the away goal rule.

We fared much better in the FA Cup. We beat Spurs and Derby to reach the fifth round, where we faced Swindon Town. A game I remember well.

I had gone up for a corner, and Swindon's Duncan Shearer and myself clashed heads. I came out worse, as he split my head open. As if that wasn't bad enough, Macca had gone for the same ball and clashed with the back of my head. Both Macca and I were on the floor for a good while being looked at by Jim Walker. We were both OK, though. After the game, the club's doctor, David Targett, came to see me and stitched me up. I think he had been enjoying Swindon's hospitality in the bar a little too much, but he soon had me right as rain. I looked awful, but Ron Atkinson always said that if a centre half doesn't come off covered in blood, they haven't done their job properly. I think it's fair to say that we had done our jobs properly in that match. We won the game 2-1.

We lost the quarter final 1-0 to eventual FA Cup winners Liverpool at Anfield. We didn't deserve to lose the match, in all fairness. I felt we deserved at least a draw and a chance to have a second crack at Villa Park in the replay, but it wasn't to be. During that match, we played in our third kit, which was yellow with the badge nearly all across the front. If my memory serves me well, I don't think we ever wore it again, and that shirt has become a bit of a collector's item.

I had just completed my first season in the top flight, playing 49 games, more than any other player with the exception of Kevin Richardson, who also played 49 times. I was playing with better players and was really pleased with the way I had contributed to the team.

Our holiday in the summer of 1992 took us to Florida. We had a great few weeks out there. Those were the days before the internet and 24-hour news channels, and when we got back to England, we realised that football had changed forever.

The summer of 1992 saw a new concept introduced: the Premier League replaced the First Division. Basically, all 24 clubs resigned from the Football League to form this new league in what became the biggest shake-up in the history of the game in England. The old Second Division became the First Division, the old Third Division became the Second Division and the fourth tier became the Third Division. There was still relegation and promotion, but to all intents and purposes, the top-flight teams had broken away from the Football Association to chase the money, with Sky TV acquiring the rights to show live football matches. The BBC were left with *Match of the Day*, with the Premier League highlights broadcast on Saturday nights.

There was a new slogan: 'A whole new ball game.' Sky produced an advert featuring a player from each of the 24 clubs, with the backing track the Simple Minds song 'Alive and Kicking'. Villa's representative was Tony Daley. All this was very new, and we were not used to all the razzamatazz, so the piss-taking with Tony was constant for a few weeks. Tony is a great lad and took it all in his stride.

Football may have been going through a major change, and there was a lot more cash flowing about, but unfortunately none of it made it into our pockets. The money took a few more years to reach the players, but it was great to have been part of the football revolution from the beginning.

Ron's second summer in charge didn't result in anywhere near as many transfers as it had in his first. Big Ron had signed Earl Barrett from Oldham towards the end of the previous season, and our biggest summer signing before the start of the 1992–1993 season was Ray Houghton. He had been a brilliant servant to Oxford United and Liverpool, and it was a good move for the Villa, as he would bolster our midfield. Ron also bought in a couple of young German players called Stefan Beinlich and Mattheus Breitkreutz. They were really good lads who lived on our estate, moving into the houses previously occupied by Ivo Stas and Kent Nielsen.

The good news was that he was keeping faith with the majority of the lads who had finished just outside the top six. I think that galvanised us and made us want to do even better.

Our first game of the Premier League era was away at Ipswich Town on a baking hot day in August. I was drenched with sweat by the end of it. Ipswich had taken the lead just on the half hour and kept it until six minutes from time, when Dalian Atkinson scored our first Premier League goal. I have the dubious honour of being the first player to be booked. It was a tackle from behind; I like to think that it was a firm but fair challenge, although the referee felt otherwise.

We then went on to draw 1-1 at home to champions Leeds, with Dalian once again on the scoresheet. We looked good for the win, but a mix-up between Macca and Spinksy resulted in Gary Speed netting the equaliser. A few days later, in another 1-1 draw, this time against Southampton, Dalian bagged his third goal in three games following an assist by new signing Frank McAvennie. Frank had been a fine striker for West Ham but was now coming to the end of his career. Big Cyrille Regis was another who could play alongside Dalian, but he was getting on in age too. Time waits for no man, as they say. Dwight Yorke was also knocking on the door, but we got the feeling that Ron didn't quite think he was ready to make the starting line-up.

There were rumblings that the boss was looking for a new striker who still had a few good years ahead of him. Pretty soon the papers were printing stories that Dean Saunders, who was playing for Liverpool at the time, was Ron's number one target.

After a loss, a win and another loss, we played Crystal Palace at home.

We still hadn't signed a striker and the Villa fans were becoming frustrated, so Ron came onto the pitch before kick-off to tell the fans to be patient with the signing of Dean Saunders. What was funny, though, was that Ron came on and pronounced Deano's surname Sanders, like Colonel Sanders from Kentucky Fried Chicken!

We won 3-0, and the Palace striker Mark Bright was lucky to leave Villa Park in one piece. Early in the game, Bright had gone in on Macca with a hard tackle. Macca felt that it was unnecessary and started to chase him around the pitch. I could see that Macca was losing it and could well get himself sent off or injured. I told him to calm down and said I would deal with it.

Soon enough, I found myself going for a high ball with Bright and I caught him with my elbow, resulting in a split to his head. This was the end of Mark Bright's participation in the match.

At the end of the game, both Bright and Macca were in the physio's room. Macca tried to get at Bright there and then, as he was still very angry, and it took a couple of us to calm him down. Looking back, I am surprised that Bright went in so hard on Macca in the first place. Every time Paul went up for the ball, he would let out this mighty roar – and I mean it was an almighty noise. It used to scare me, let alone the opposition!

Ron finally got his man a few days after the Palace game, with Dean Saunders joining us for £2.3 million, a record for the Villa at the time. This was a big signing and made the rest of the Premier League sit up and take note.

Deano made his home debut in a memorable game against his old club, Liverpool. It was a great match that produced one of the greatest misses of all time – and the most relieved person on the pitch when it happened was me!

The game was played in front of 38,000 fans, and the tempo was high right from kick-off. However, despite the tempo, neither side was able to score. Then, with a couple of minutes to go until half-time, the game took on a new dimension. David James, Liverpool's goalkeeper, played a long ball up into our half. I was marking Ronny Rosenthal. I was deceived by the long clearance by James, and the Israeli forward nipped in behind me. I tried in vain to catch Ronny, shouting all sorts at him, desperately trying to make amends for my blunder. I told him that he was an awful footballer and that he was bound to miss, and I did it in a high-pitched voice, as I was so desperate.

Ronny rounded Nigel Spink and the open goal presented itself. Then, amazingly, he thrashed his shot goal against the bar from just five yards out before being cleared by Earl Barrett. I drew breath and dusted myself down. Unfortunately, the right side of my brain didn't receive the memo from my left, and I was soon making another mistake. This time Liverpool did take advantage. I miscalculated the ball, which allowed David Burrows to fire the ball in for Mark Walters to score. I was so mad with myself, but luckily Deano equalised on his debut. The Holte End, and the rest of the stadium, erupted. I felt so happy, as I hated knowing that I had let the team down. At half-time, the lads told me not to worry and to just concentrate on the second half. Deano scored his second goal, and we ended up winning the game 4-2.

That result was the first time in the season when we felt we could actually achieve something special. We had kept the nucleus of the team from the previous campaign, and our new signings had added real quality. Just how far could we go was the question.

Before the next league game, we beat Oxford United 2-1 in the League Cup. What made it special was that our goals were scored by me and Macca. They both came from corners. Macca got the first when he calmly headed home after Oxford had failed to clear the ball. My goal came from the left-hand side. The ball came to me and I hit it goal bound. It took a deflection and sailed into the net. I was interviewed by the *Birmingham Evening Mail* after the game and this is what I said:

> When you score as infrequently as me, you take anything that comes along. My shot was going in the far corner, but it hit someone on the knee and the keeper got a hand to it and knocked it in the other side. But as far as I'm concerned it was my goal because the ball was going in anyway.

The next two games were tough away fixtures against Middlesbrough and Wimbledon, but we made it three away wins on the trot with two 3-2 victories. Deano continued his fine start in Villa colours with a brace at Ayresome Park. Dalian scored the other. I could see straight away that both players were going to form a great partnership. It was déjà vu at Wimbledon, with Deano again scoring two goals and Dalian bagging the other. It was Dalian's goal that took all the plaudits that day – a goal that was shown all around the world. It still is to this day. It won the Goal of the Season and remains one of the best individual goals ever scored. Again, the *Birmingham Evening Mail* came up trumps with their write-up on the goal. At the time we were somewhat under the cosh when Dalian won the ball.

> Villa scored one of the goals of the season when Atkinson picked up the ball ten yards inside his own half. He shrugged off three tackles on his way to goal and finished with an inch perfect chip over Hans Segers.

I was directly behind Dalian and basically ran behind him all the way. My initial thought was for him to release the ball and then make his way into the penalty area for the return ball, but as he evaded tackle after tackle, I could sense something special was going to happen. I saw him chip the keeper and I ran towards Dalian. If you watch the footage, you'll notice that I'm one of the players that got under the famous umbrella shot when one of our fans (a.k.a. Rain Man) got on the pitch to celebrate that wonderful moment. The rain did nothing to dampen the spirits of the players and the fans that day. The win moved us into fifth place in the league.

It was back to League Cup duty next with the return leg against Oxford, and we won the game 2-1 again. Macca didn't play, but I did. I had taken enough of the limelight from the first leg, so I allowed Dalian and Rico to score against Oxford. The team unity was strengthening match by match.

Our next fixture was against big spending Blackburn Rovers. Jack Walker was a local businessman and the owner of the club that he loved and had bankrolled then in a bid to become successful. They had just bought Alan Shearer for a British record fee and they were beginning to look the part. The game was chosen as the Monday night live game on Sky. It was like being part of American football with the loud music and dancing girls; however, the game didn't live up to the billing and finished goalless. Blackburn were in second place, and we were now in fourth.

Our fine run continued throughout October and November as we picked up two 1-0 wins at Villa Park, both against Manchester United, one in the League Cup and one in the league.

Our first defeat in 14 games came on 28 November at home against high-flying Norwich City. It was a great game for the purists, as the Canaries won 3-2 in a pulsating match. I didn't actually play in the game, as I was injured, but believe me when I say that I kicked every ball. The win saw Norwich go top and we remained in fourth place.

We soon got back to winning ways with wins against Sheffield Wednesday and Nottingham Forest, although we crashed out of the League Cup with a defeat at Ipswich Town and then lost 3-0 to Coventry City on Boxing Day, with big Micky Quinn taking the match ball home with a hat-trick. Our final game of 1992 saw us beat Arsenal 1-0 at home, and we finished the year in third place behind Manchester United and Norwich, who remained in top spot.

The top three changed hands several times during the second half of the season. We began the New Year as we had finished the last, with two great wins. Firstly, we beat Liverpool 2-1 at Anfield to complete the double over them, and then we thrashed Middlesbrough 5-1 at Villa Park to complete another double. The deadly duo – no, not Dalian and Deano – were once again amongst the goals, with Macca scoring the second and yours truly bagging the fifth. It was a real team effort that night, as we had five different scorers, Garry Parker, Yorkie and Deano the other names on the scoresheet. That win took us up to second place.

In the FA Cup we saw off the challenge of Bristol Rovers, beating them in a replay. Malcolm Allison, the Rovers manager, had stoked things up in the press before the match, telling them that Rovers were going to do this and that to us. They didn't, though. Unlucky Malc.

We eventually went out of the FA Cup in the fourth round, losing to Wimbledon on penalties. Rico took a kick and absolutely skied it. I am not sure the ball has even landed yet! I would like to place on record that I did once again convert mine!

We moved to the top of the league for the first time on Saturday 13 February 1993, following a 1-0 win at Chelsea with a Ray Houghton goal. We had played some great football previously, but against Chelsea we had our backs against the wall for long periods of the match and we nicked the win. I guess you could say we showed true grit that day. We only had a two-point lead, and with Manchester United and Norwich both having games over us, we knew we couldn't afford to be complacent.

We then lost the lead after a goalless stalemate at Villa Park against Spurs. We did everything but score, and Deano hit the bar and the post. We dropped to second behind United but only on goals scored.

Then it was the big one away at Old Trafford, which was beamed live around the world via Sky. We drew the game 1-1, with Stan Staunton scoring a rocket to give us the lead before Mark Hughes equalised for the home team. Norwich capitalised with a win to go into top spot. I picked up a booking in the United match as well. I knew I had to be careful, because we were well and truly in a serious title battle and I didn't want to miss a single minute of the action. The trouble was that it was not in my nature to go into a tackle with anything less than 100%. I knew the risks and so did Ron.

A 2-0 home win against Sheffield Wednesday saw us reclaim second place. Dalian had picked up an injury, and Dwight came into the side and scored both goals. His first came in within a couple of minutes of kick-off, which really helped to settle the nerves. It was a beautifully worked team goal which ended up with Yorkie sliding in at the back post. I must have been the only one that didn't touch the ball during that passage of play.

The following match was another six pointer when we travelled to Carrow Road for a mid-week game against Norwich. We lost the game 1-0 and they moved back to the top of the table.

We won 1-0 at Nottingham Forest in the next game, with Macca scoring the all-important goal with a bullet header from a corner to claim top spot with just seven games to go. Another bonus was that Dalian was fit again and came off the bench to replace Big Cyrille.

Then, on Saturday 10 April, everything changed in the title race and the pendulum swung very favourably towards Alex Ferguson and Manchester United. We played Coventry at home, and United were entertaining Sheffield Wednesday. Much like the Spurs game, we threw everything but the kitchen sink at Coventry, and Deano continued his love affair with the woodwork. The game finished goalless, but as we got into the dressing room, we found out that Manchester United were losing 1-0 and the match was in injury time. This gave us a boost in the dressing room until we found out that United had not only equalised deep into stoppage time but had actually gone on to win the game. Steve Bruce scored both goals with headers in what became known as Fergie Time. We sat in the dressing room in absolute shock. It had been nearly 10 minutes since we had walked off the pitch and Manchester United had played on. That seemed to have put an extra spring into United's step, and from that moment on, they didn't lose top spot.

We continued to win games, such as away at Arsenal and at home to United's rivals, Manchester City. I didn't play in the City game, as I had picked up one too many bookings. That was the risk I was taking for my no-nonsense approach, as I have stated previously. I was invited to watch the game in the Sky studio in the Holte End and be a pundit for this live game. We won 3-1. Two things stood out for me that day. One, there was a large banner in the City end that was in support of us winning the league title. Anyone but United in the eyes of City fans. The other thing was a handball committed by Keith Curle that gave us a penalty. It was so strange, as there was absolutely no need for him to raise his hands. I looked at Richard Keys in the studio and it was a good job there were no microphones on, because he shouted, "What the fuck has he done there?"

We were not complaining, though, as Garry Parker converted the spot kick. It was still advantage United, but the win meant we were still in with a chance. Norwich had dropped points, having lost to Manchester United at home, so they were pretty much out of the title race.

We had three matches remaining, and all three were must-win games. The first of these was away at Blackburn Rovers. Dalian Atkinson had come back into the team after his layoff but perhaps wasn't as sharp as he had been before his injury. He missed a golden chance to put us in front in the first couple of minutes. Football can be a cruel mistress, and we found ourselves 3-0 down by half-time. There was to be no comeback, and that's how the game finished. United's first championship in 26 years was confirmed on Sunday 2 May when we lost at home to Oldham Athletic 1-0. The Latics still had something to play for, as they were battling relegation. They simply wanted it more than us that day, and the victory helped them to stay up.

In the final game of the season, we played Queens Park Rangers and lost 2-1. Loftus Road was full of Villa fans who had come down in their thousands to cheer us on, and whilst the season ended in disappointment, we still had a lot to cheer about. The relationship between the fans and the players was just great that day.

United finished the season 10 points above us with 84 points. There was no way that they were that many points better than us, though. We had taken four points off them in the league and knocked them out of the League Cup. They had Lady Luck on their side at times, like the Fergie Time win against Sheffield

Wednesday, and we lost Dalian Atkinson to injury at the wrong time. That is not taking anything away from them. They went on a winning run at just the right time, and Fergie had brought in Eric Cantona in the winter from Leeds, and he had made a massive difference to the team.

We had gone from being the seventh best team in the land to becoming the second best in the first season of the Sky football revolution. Now we were being talked about as a serious contender. The question was, could we live up to it as the 1993–1994 season beckoned?

The answer was a *no* in the league but a firm *yes* in the League Cup.

Again, Ron kept faith with the nucleus of the team that had come so close to winning the league. He made two significant signings to bolster the squad for the new season. Andy Townsend joined from Chelsea and Guy Whittingham was signed from Portsmouth. Andy had such a dark sense of humour but would make us laugh. Garry Parker and Dean Saunders were the jokers in the pack, but now we had Andy as well. In contrast, Guy was a quiet lad who kept himself to himself. There was no denying his goal-scoring prowess, though, as he had banged in around 40 goals for Pompey in one season. Guy had taken himself out of the army to play for Pompey, and whilst he didn't score anywhere near the number of goals he had done on the south coast, he still chipped in with some important goals for us.

We started the season on fire with a 4-1 home victory over Queens Park Rangers. That gave us a little bit of revenge after we had lost to them in the last game of the previous season. Andy fitted in well to our midfield and the team gelled straight away, which gave us the bounce we needed after the disappointing finish to the previous campaign. We drew the next couple of games against Sheffield Wednesday and Wimbledon away, so it was a solid start.

Then it was our first Monday night live game of the campaign – a match that was being billed as a potential title decider even though it was only the fourth game of the season: Aston Villa against Manchester United. I don't need to tell you how much this game meant to us, and we were hellbent on taking revenge on them. Perhaps we focused too much on the revenge part in the end, as we lost the game 2-1. United played in an all-black strip on the night. Lee Sharpe scored both goals and ended up serenading the corner flag in his Elvis pose – it certainly had us all shook up!

We then went on a great run, winning eight of the next eleven matches, losing just once to Newcastle United. During that run we played Oldham at Boundary Park. We failed to score in the first half and missed some chances. Ron was furious as we got into the dressing room at half-time and was questioning why we hadn't scored. He was pointing at Dean Saunders, who seemed to be in his firing line. Whether it was meant or not, Ron threw his hot tea in the direction of Deano. Luckily the vast majority missed, but nevertheless, Deano was furious. I honestly thought Deano was going to punch Ron at the time. It obviously stoked him up, as he was on the scoresheet in the second half to secure us a 1-1 draw.

One time things did spill over was when we played Chelsea away and drew 1-1. Deano scored our goal, but Dalian missed a really good chance to give us the lead. Ron was so mad that he subbed Dalian soon after. Dalian was furious with himself, not only for the miss but also because he'd been subbed and hadn't had a proper chance to redeem himself. It came to a head after the match when Dalian was in the shower. Ron couldn't let his miss go and followed Dalian into the showers. Ron was fully dressed, so imagine our surprise when both squared up to each other in the showers! It took intervention from myself, Andy Townsend and Rico to calm the two Atkinsons down. Jim Barron stood on the side and barked out orders that under no circumstance should this story get out in the media. I can confirm right here and now that I never said a word, but the next morning I was reading about it in one of the nationals! To this day, we don't know who leaked the story.

I scored my first ever away Premier League goal in a 2-1 win over Swindon Town at the end of October 1993, and we followed that up with two more wins, against Arsenal and Sheffield United. Those victories meant we sat in second place behind Manchester United, who had been top since they beat us earlier in the season. Was history about to repeat itself? Or could we go one better and pip them to the title?

Unfortunately, that was when it all started to go wrong for us. Second place was as good as it got for Villa in the Premier League that season.

We won just once in our next eight league games. A seven-match unbeaten run early in 1994 made us think we'd turned a corner, but it proved to be a false dawn.

The only positive for us was our cup exploits.

Our reward for finishing second the previous season was qualification for the UEFA Cup, so I was able to experience continental football for the first time. We beat ŠK Slovan Bratislava 2-1 on aggregate but then went out by the same score to the Spanish team Deportivo La Coruña. It was very disappointing, because we had picked up a useful 1-1 draw in Spain before losing 1-0 at Villa Park.

I have already told you about our exploits in the FA Cup in the first chapter of this book. You also know that we reached the semi-final of the 1994 League Cup, which was sponsored by Coca-Cola that season. But how did we reach the semi-final and what happened in the final?

We were drawn against Birmingham City in the second round. At the time, I didn't know just how big the rivalry between the two clubs was, but I certainly did afterwards. In the first leg we beat Blues 1-0 at St Andrew's, with Rico scoring the goal. The atmosphere was absolutely red hot and in many ways it was a cauldron of hate, as it had been a few seasons since both teams had met. We had the better chances, but it could have been so different if Birmingham's John Frain had scored his penalty, which was saved by Mark Bosnich. Nigel Spink had started in goal for us but picked up an injury and was replaced by Bozzie. When he saved it, we all went up to congratulate him, but he was far too busy giving it to the Blues fans behind the goal!

We won the second leg 1-0 at Villa Park. Rico was in the thick of it once more, as he was pushed into the crowd by Birmingham's Paul Tait, who was sent off. Blues were down to 10-men, although at times you wouldn't have thought so, as they gave it a real good go. Deano scored the winning goal for us, although at the time there was some controversy, as Birmingham thought he was offside.

It was then off to Roker Park to play Sunderland in the third round. We won 4-1, but our goalkeeper was Man of the Match. Bozzie had retained his place in the starting line-up, and the simple fact is that if we hadn't had him in goal that night, we would not have won. Although the Black Cats did score one, they could and should have scored a lot more. Bozzie was outstanding that night, making save after save. Sunderland were relentless from the get-go, and we knew we'd been in a game by the time the final whistle went. They ran us ragged, but we won and that was all that mattered.

We then received another away draw for the fourth round, against the holders, Arsenal. We came away with a 1-0 win, although it was far more comfortable than the scoreline suggests.

Our reward for that victory was another away game, this time against Tottenham Hotspur. Ugo played in defence one and held his own. Sol Campbell was playing up front for Spurs and had given them the lead before going off – fortunately for us. We won the game 2-1.

As for Tranmere in the semi-final, well, I've given my account already. It simply was one of the greatest two-legged semi-final matches of all time.

And so on to the final itself, held in March 1994, and the build-up to what is famously known as Wembley Week. It was not without incident from the Monday right through to the Saturday afternoon, which was just 24 hours before we kicked off against Manchester United. United had taken top spot in the league as early as the fourth game of the season and never looked back. It was just a case of *when* they would be crowned champions again, not *if*. They were also motoring in the FA Cup and the treble was on. They were red-hot favourites coming into the League Cup final.

On the Monday it was photoshoot time when we went out to be measured for our cup final suits. We all went to Ciro Citterio, an Italian designer menswear shop in Birmingham. At that time, it was one of the most popular retail stores, certainly in the Midlands. Some of the boys – Dalian and Deano – were very vocal in their opinion that they wanted us to wear something more haute couture like Armani or Hugo Boss. It was funny watching them trying to remove the logo from the inside pocket. I had come from non-league, and I would have been happy with anything at that time, as I'd never owned a suit before. The fact that the club were giving me designer gear was amazing.

We trained as normal at Bodymoor Heath on the Tuesday and Wednesday. On Thursday, it was time for us to travel down to London. We were stopping at the Royal Lancaster Hotel near Hyde Park. The club felt that it would be good for the players and staff to have a night together with their partners, as it would be good for morale. It certainly was. Just being able to room with our loved ones was a huge positive. We all went out for an Italian meal with Ron and his wife, Maggie. We were allowed to have a couple of drinks, and it was a really nice relaxing evening. The next morning it was down to the serious business of preparing for the cup final. I said goodbye to Carol and then we were transported to our hotel at Bisham Abbey in Marlow, just outside London, where we would be staying until after the final. The hotel was frequently used by cup finalists.

We trained on the Friday and then it was time for some lighter training on the Saturday. No one wanted to get hurt and put themselves in real danger of missing the match. Ron had decided that United would be dangerous at set pieces, so we set up to practise corners. I cannot remember who put the cross in, but I went up for the ball, as did Mark Bosnich. Both of us missed the ball, which was a real shame, as Bozzie followed through and punched me square on the nose. The other lads heard the crack of my nose as I fell to the floor with blood gushing down my face. It was just 24 hours from the biggest game of my life and I had broken my nose!

There was no way that that injury – or any, for that matter – was going to make me miss the final, though. My nose started to swell a bit and I took some time out. Shortly after the training session finished, Ron called us all into a room individually to tell us whether we'd made the team. Here is what happened when it was my turn:

Ron: Alright, Tealey. How's the nose, son?
Me: Alright, gaffer.
Ron: Feeling fit, then?
Me: Yes, gaffer.
Ron: OK, you're starting the match.
Me: Cheers, gaffer.

And that was it. I was going to play in the League Cup final. At Wembley.

Back in March of 1974, I was playing for my school team, sitting on a radiator in the dressing room, getting chilblains from the cold.

In March 1984, I was playing non-league football for my hometown club after bring rejected from Everton.

Now, in March 1994, I was playing in the Premier League and was about to step onto the pitch at Wembley to play a major cup final against one of the biggest clubs in the world in front of nearly 100,000 people, with millions watching on TV around the world. I felt so proud of where I had come from, especially the fact that I never gave up on my dream.

But we had a job to do, so there was no room for sentiment.

We had breakfast together on the morning of the final and went for a stroll; some of the lads went back to their rooms to get some more sleep or just relax.

Then it was time to board the team coach for the short trip to Wembley Stadium. Joining us on the coach that day was the comedian Stan Boardman, who was a close friend of Ron's. This was the first time I had seen him perform, although I'd been told that he just repeated old jokes. However, I found him quite funny, to be fair, and had a good laugh on the way in. We soon made our way to the famous old stadium with the Twin Towers and then we found ourselves on the pitch, wearing our Ciro Citterio suits.

The United players were also on the pitch, taking in the atmosphere. I was standing near the centre circle with Earl Barrett when three United players, Bryan Robson, Paul Ince and Lee Sharpe, came over for a quick chat. We shook hands and then the topic of conversation moved on to my larger than normal nose. "Fucking hell, Tealey," said Sharpie. I knew him really well and we were mates in the game. "How the fuck did that happen?"

They all stood there laughing. I told them about the incident with Bozzie and they just carried on laughing. They couldn't believe that I was still playing. It was all good banter.

But then it was back to the battle ahead as we went our separate ways and walked back into our dressing rooms.

Our line-up for the final was:

Goalkeeper: Mark Bosnich.
Defence: Earl Barrett, Steve Staunton, Shaun Teale, Paul McGrath,
Midfield: Kevin Richardson, Andy Townsend, Graham Fenton, Dalian Atkinson, Tony Daley,
Attack: Dean Saunders.

Ron informed us that we would be playing a 4-5-1 formation. The surprise choice was Graham Fenton, who had only played a few games, but Ron felt that he would link up well with Andy Townsend, just behind Dean Saunders, with Rico sitting in and Dalian and Tony on the flanks. Ron had called me over in the morning and gently reminded me that a month earlier, Steve Staunton had had a hernia operation, and he asked me to look out for him on that left side. It went without saying that I would cover for him, but I made a joke about making sure I marked Ryan Giggs and Eric Cantona out of the game as well as covering for Stan!

The nerves had started to kick in by now. Some of the lads just sat there in quiet contemplation; others were preparing in their own way. We were then called to the tunnel area, and that was when the adrenaline started to set in for me. I had only been to Wembley for schoolboy matches during the 1970s, but this was very different. I couldn't help but soak it all in.

The game itself started at a frenetic pace, with United asking questions of our defence before we got into the match. When we did, we were able to draw first blood.

In the 26th minute Deano put the ball over to Dalian, who ran into the box and coolly slotted the it home past my old smoking partner, Les Sealey.

I didn't take playing at Wembley for granted that day, but I knew I had to play the match, not the occasion. It's a well-used phrase in football, but it's true. So much so that most of our defenders didn't rush up to congratulate Dalian. We wanted to keep our shape and maintain focus. The slaps on the back would happen in the dressing room at half-time. Which they did, as the score remained 1-0.

I looked at Macca and we both agreed we needed more of the same in the second half. We all had to be on top of our game as the second half progressed and United came at us. Our tackling at the back was just quality that day.

We went two up with 70 minutes on the clock from a free kick that we had practised. It actually went better for us on the day than it had in training. The ball went into the box and Deano stuck his foot out and put the ball into the net.

We still had 20 minutes to go, and we knew that despite the two-lead cushion, United were a force to be reckoned with and could still get back into the game. But we defended so well that even though United looked threatening on the ball and had the majority of the possession, they had no real clear-cut chances.

Even when they pulled a goal back with seven minutes to go, we continued to restrict them to just one further chance. Don't get me wrong, we didn't sit back and defend; we played the game like it was still up for grabs.

With just minutes to go we got a penalty after Tony Daley smashed the ball against the post, and then Dalian followed up with a goal-bound shot only for Andrei Kanchelskis to stop it with his hands. We knew that if we converted it, we could relax and enjoy the last few minutes. Up stepped Deano, who put the ball away to make it 3-1. We were in dreamland.

I looked at Macca and we smiled at each other. No words were needed. United had put ball after ball into the box and we had dealt with them every time. We knew we had done our jobs.

When the referee blew the final whistle, the next 10 minutes or so were just a blur. I couldn't stop smiling at the lads. There was a pile-on and back slapping galore. There is a saying in football that Wembley is no place for losers, and I agree. I'm glad I didn't get to experience that.

As we climbed up to the Royal Box, I looked down at each step I was taking, making sure I remembered each one and taking everything in. I watched Rico pick up the cup, lift it high in the air and with that, all eyes turned towards the thousands of fans with their arms raised inside the stadium. It was a wonderful sight. With my medal in my hand, I joined the rest of the team on the pitch to celebrate with our fans and drink champagne. We did the usual laps of honour, and each of us took turns holding the cup and running up to our fans to show them what we had won. The music was blaring out loud and proud – and that was exactly how I felt.

We got back into the dressing room, showered and got changed back into our suits to meet up with our friends and families back at the Royal Lancaster Hotel for further celebrations. The last time we were there, a few days before the final, we had been told that we could only have a couple of drinks. Now it was all bets off. We could drink what we wanted – it was party time. And boy, did we do it well! I did try to get Carol to come to bed early, as I was knackered, but she was having none of it. So my plans of being in bed by 10 p.m. were completely curtailed. I think we eventually went up at 5 a.m.

Stan Boardman got up for half an hour or so. Now I fully understood why the lads were saying he repeated his jokes, because that was all he did. Garry Parker was heckling him all the way through. Garry was actually funnier than Stan on the night, just like we had been better than Manchester United on the day.

We had won the cup, and everything was just great.

Although we could look forward to another European adventure in the 1994–1995 season, our finish in the league campaign after the cup final was not great at all. Cracks in our general play had started to surface.

We won just two of our final 12 games, including a 5-1 defeat to Newcastle at St James' Park, and finished 10th in the league. What made it worse was that game cost me a chance of getting into the England team.

I had been named in a provisional squad for some summer games that had been arranged for Terry Venables' team. England had failed to make the 1994 World Cup in the United States, so the FA tried to keep the squad busy by arranging some friendlies to be played at Wembley.

During the first half, I went for a 50/50 ball with Andy Cole, and he clattered into me, mainly the back of my calf. I immediately knew something was up and I hobbled off. It turned out to be my Achilles.

I was still hopeful I could recover in time, but Ron Atkinson had already informed Terry Venables that I should be pulled out of the squad. I was gutted. Basically, Ron didn't give me the chance to at least try to recover in time for those games. I felt I could have made it, but Ron had already pulled the trigger. My teammates Earl Barrett and Kevin Richardson had also been picked and went on to play in the friendlies.

At the end of the season, we had three games to play as part of a tour of South Africa, and I was picked to go. I asked Ron why he had deemed me unfit to play for England but named me for a meaningless tournament in South Africa. I didn't get a straight answer, so in the end I just got on with it.

We flew to Johannesburg, and on the plane Ron turned to me and told me I would be captain for the duration of the trip while Rico was away with England. We played Liverpool at Ellis Park and lost 1-0. There must have been about 80,000 in the crowd.

I may not have been with the England squad, but I was captain of Aston Villa when we were introduced to the late, great Nelson Mandela. It was such an honour for me to introduce my teammates to him, and that memory will stay with me forever. Everywhere we went, we were accompanied by armed guards – in the bars and restaurants, even on the golf courses. We played a further two games in South Africa and then flew back home.

By this time cracks in my relationship with Ron Atkinson had also begun to appear.

Firstly, there was the Wembley suit saga. As I've mentioned, a few of the players had made comments that United would be arriving at the final dressed in the best designer suits, while we would be wearing Ciro Citterio. Up to that point I hadn't owned a suit before, and wearing designer clothes wasn't really my style. I preferred to stop in with Carol and the kids, and I'm sure I would have got sauce on my Hugo Boss suit when I made the kids some chips!

When I got home from the photoshoot, I gave the suit to Carol, who did no more than iron out the shirt that came with it, and then she hung it up, where it stayed until cup final day. That, to me and Carol, was the end of it – or so we thought.

It transpired that Ron had heard about Deano and Dalian's complaints that the suits weren't designer. While it had been said as a joke, they were also making a serious point. For some reason he thought that Carol had instigated it all. Whilst nothing was said at the time, looking back and unbeknown to me, this was the start of the deterioration of our relationship. I really wish Ron had spoken to me or Carol and we could have put him right. I get that all his thoughts were on the final and the football side and the last thing he needed was stress about what suits the players were wearing, but we could have set the record straight.

Carol agreed: "It did upset me that Ron thought I was somehow responsible for the turmoil about the suits and that he maybe thought I was something of a bad influence. I wish he would have spoken to me about it, though. He gave absolutely no indication that there was an issue. Ron and Maggie held a summer party just before the start of the 1994–1995 season. It was a lovely day and Ron shouted to me, 'Tealey, open up another bottle of champers.' It was a really good laugh. So to see me name checked negatively in one of his later books was very disappointing, to say the least."

Whilst I had gone along with the South Africa visit, in the back of my mind I was still a little miffed that Ron had deemed me fit for this tour but hadn't allowed me to fulfil my dream of playing for England.

On the plane home from South Africa, I spoke with Jim Walker about what I needed to get done so that I would be fighting fit for my fourth season with the Villa. Jim agreed that I needed to get my nose done and also that I would require a double hernia operation on my groin. I should have had the first one done during the first part of the cup-winning season, but it was Ron's view that they could wait until the summer break, which seemed strange when you think that he had allowed Stan Staunton to have his done a month or so before the League Cup final. I didn't make anything of it, though, as we had the final to prepare for, so I put it to the back of my mind.

Once Jim had agreed, he called Ron over to go through what we had discussed. Ron's words to me on the plane were, "Take the extra two weeks that the Irish lads are having. Have the ops done, and we will see you back then."

I was happy with that arrangement. The Irish lads were participating in the 1994 World Cup, even if England were not. It meant that I could have the hernia operation down in Harley Street, London, get my nose done a little closer to home in Little Aston, just outside Sutton Coldfield, and have a bit of time to relax with my family. The ops and having a couple of weeks away was just what I needed to prepare myself mentally and physically for the season ahead. This meant that I would miss the start of pre-season training, which was being held at an army camp down south. Even if I hadn't been given special dispensation, like Macca and the boys, I still would not have made the army camp because of my operation.

Our family holiday was in Florida and the kids loved it. One night we were walking around the Disney marketplace and we bumped into Ron and Maggie. They were the last people we thought we would see. Maggie said hello to Carol and the boys, but Ron walked past and blanked me. Carol made a comment that Ron had been rude and I told her not to worry about it and not to let it spoil our holiday. In the back of my mind, though, I was wondering why he had done it. We had a great holiday, returned to Birmingham and forgot about the incident with Ron.

I knew the lads were getting ready to travel down south for boot camp, as I had spoken to one or two of them on the phone. I then received a phone call from Jim Barron asking me where I was and why I wasn't at boot camp. My initial thought was that Jim had got his wires crossed, but I was a little concerned that he kept repeating that Ron had asked him to call me. I told Jim in no uncertain terms that there was no way I was joining up with them, as I had had two operations that required rest and I couldn't go even if I wanted to. Jim knew there was nothing more he could do and put the phone down.

I decided that I would head off to Bodymoor Heath and see who was around, but the lads had already departed by the time I got there. I caught up with one of the physios, and he agreed to do some one-on-one training with me to get me back up to a decent fitness level while it was quiet. Not only did I want to do this, but I felt it would look good to Ron. This training carried on for the week, and they were pretty good sessions.

Then, on the last day before the lads were due back, I went into Bodymoor Heath to do my usual training. I got changed and as I was walking down the corridor, I saw Ron coming towards me. He must have left boot camp early to get prepared for the lads' return. Just like he had done in Florida, he walked past me and didn't even acknowledge that I was there. Now I knew we had a serious issue. I honestly thought that me coming in to train would make him see that I was being proactive about my recovery.

The lads came back, and we got back into pre-season training. I continued my one-on-one sessions. I wanted to speak to Jim Walker about what had happened on the phone with Jim Barron and the snub by Ron. I couldn't believe it when he said that he didn't remember having the conversation with me and Ron on the plane. I could tell he was feeling uncomfortable. Here was a guy that I trusted just like the other players did. I told Jim just how unhappy I was, and he wouldn't look at me. Shortly afterwards, I was called into Ron's office. There were no handshakes or hellos. "Where were you, Shaun? You should have been at boot camp," he asked.

I was fuming inside but decided to be professional. I firmly but fairly pointed out that all this had been agreed on the plane home from South Africa. At first, he denied the conversation had ever taken place. After some toing and froing, Ron admitted that the conversation had taken place. Then he said, "Yeah we did agree to it, but that changed when I saw you on holiday in Florida."

I couldn't believe what he was saying. The holiday had been booked before the operations, and I pointed out that surely it was best to have the holiday and then fully recuperate at home. Ron was having none of it, though. All he could see was that I had gone away on holiday and nothing else. I left his office with nothing really resolved.

I knew what was coming, as I had been in football for a long time. I wasn't selected for any of the pre-season games. Instead, Ron partnered Macca with Ugo. I was on the bench for the first game of the season, which was away at Everton. This was also the case for the next five games of the season. I was an unused substitute in the San Siro for our UEFA Cup tie against Inter Milan. We lost the game 1-0.

However, I was back in the team and actually kicking a ball in anger in the very next match against West Ham, which we won 1-0. It had been a solid start in the league for Villa, with three wins and three draws from the first six matches, so it was looking good for the team. I was in and out of the team for the next few matches and then once again dropped from the match day squad.

By then the team were not playing brilliantly and results had started to drop, but when selected, I played my part and gave 100%, as I always did. The results were getting worse, and by the time we lost 2-1 to Manchester United at home in November 1994, we were in the bottom three.

We had beaten United just a few months earlier in the final, of course, but now they were miles ahead of us. I desperately wanted to get onto that pitch and rectify the situation. They were my teammates, and I hated to see their faces in training after yet another defeat. My relationship with Ron had now broken down completely. It was so sad after everything we had been through, but I knew that I needed to play, especially at my age, so I reluctantly submitted a transfer request. It was the last resort, but I felt it had to be done.

Ron put a £3 million bounty on my head. We both knew that no club would pay that, but again it was Ron thinking he had all the cards.

Another incident happened with Ron that was totally unnecessary in my view. Carol had decided that she was going to spring clean the house from top to bottom and move things around. I had just finished training and when I got home, she asked me to move the fish tank. I did no more than pick it up and for some reason it just shattered. We were able to save the fish straight away, which was a good thing. The bad thing was that I cut my wrists open and blood was spurting everywhere. Carol drove me to Good Hope Hospital in Sutton Coldfield to get it cleared up. It took a couple of visits and little operations to get it fixed. When this got back to Ron, I heard that he made comments that Carol had tried to stab me! Why would he say such a thing? It was just another incident that proved he no longer wanted me at the club, but his valuation of me meant that I would not get many takers.

Matters on the pitch were getting worse, and it came to a head in the next game at Wimbledon on Wednesday 9 November. As was the norm by then, I wasn't named in the squad. We went

3-1 up just after half-time and looked good for the win until the Dons pulled it back to 3-3 and then won the game with a minute to go. Future Villa midfielder Øyvind Leonhardsen scored the winner for Wimbledon.

That defeat was too much to bear for Villa chairman Doug Ellis and the board, and it was very quickly announced that Ron would be leaving the club. We'd lost eight of the past nine games and were very much locked into a relegation battle. I actually found out that Ron had been sacked via teletext. For the younger readers, that was our version of Google in the early part of the 1990s. Ask your parents!

I shouted the news to Carol, who was upstairs, and we shouted the house down in delight. After everything that had happened, yes, I was really pleased to see him go!

The last thing we wanted to do was leave Villa. We loved the place and it had become our home. Well, a home as much as a footballer can have one, I guess. I knew that Doug Ellis had not travelled to the Wimbledon game, so we got one of the neighbours to look after the kids and we went round to his house – well, mansion – which wasn't that far. Heidi, Doug's wife, answered the door and said hello. I asked if I could see the chairman.

"Of course," she replied. She was a lovely woman and always had time for the players and their wives. Doug was in his study. He looked very tired, and you could tell he had just come off the phone.

I asked him where I stood. I really didn't want to leave the club, and I told the chairman how I felt.

"Don't worry, Shaun. I can't tell you who will be the next manager yet, but I can tell you that you are in his plans," was all Doug said. That was music to my ears, and I shook the chairman's hand and we said our goodbyes to Mr and Mrs Ellis and went back home.

The next morning, the first thing I did was ask to come off the transfer list. Bodymoor Heath was a busy place for the next few days. Ron came in to collect all his stuff, and Jim Barron was walking around like a lost puppy. The players were all called into a meeting, and when we got there, we were surprised to see Jim giving the talk. He basically blamed the players for the mess we had gotten ourselves into and said it was nothing to do with him or Ron!

A couple of days later, it was announced that the prodigal son was returning to Villa Park. Brian Little was a legend at the club long before he was appointed as Ron's replacement. He had played for the club in the 1970s and was widely regarded as one of the best players to have worn the claret and blue of Aston Villa. He had taken Leicester City into the Premier League but left the Foxes to return to Aston Villa. His first away game in charge was . . . yes, against Leicester at Filbert Street. Just like Ron's first away game was against his former club.

It was a red-hot atmosphere at Filbert Street for the game on 3 December, although it wasn't quite as intimidating as it had been at Hillsborough back in 1991. True to Doug's word, the new manager picked me, and I took my place in the centre of defence in a game that finished 1-1. It was my first start in 12 games. It was a hard-fought point, but it left both teams still in the drop zone.

I liked Brian from the get-go, and I felt that the slate had been wiped clean. After Brian's arrival, I played in every game for the remainder of the season. I was back in the team alongside Macca in the middle of defence, I was enjoying my football again and I even assisted with a couple of goals – a 2-1 defeat at Southampton, where Ray Houghton scored, and a 1-1 draw at home against Manchester City, with Ugo scoring the goal.

We had some crazy games at Villa Park, where two matches resulted in eight goals being scored. The first was a 7-1 home win against Wimbledon. Tommy Johnson, a recent signing, scored a hat-trick and was then sick on the pitch! And then there was a 4-4 draw against Leicester City. We were furious at the end of this game, as we had been 4-1 up with just 10 minutes or so to go.

If we had won that game, I honestly don't think our relegation battle would have gone down to the wire. But it did.

We picked up a point at Norwich City, and our relegation rivals Crystal Palace lost 3-2 to Newcastle United. We had secured our Premier League status for another season. There was a massive sigh of relief. Brian and his two assistants, John Gregory and Allan Evans, had pulled it off. They were all ex-

Villa players who knew the club inside and out, and they had made training fun and interesting once more.

However, it turned out that the Norwich game would be the last time I played for Aston Villa. When Brian had first come in, he had mentioned to my agent, Phil Smith, that I would be offered a new contract. I guess Brian's mind was fully focused on retaining Premier League status for the Villa. I fully got that and patiently waited until we had officially stayed up before expecting my new contract offer. Carol and I took the boys away on holiday for a few days at the end of the season, and when we got back, I received a call from Phil, who told me that Brian Little wanted to meet. Brian informed us that he wanted to sign Chris Coleman from newly relegated Crystal Palace. Chris played in my position and the deal looked like it was going to happen. Brian explained that he could not guarantee me first team football at the club. I was 31, not getting any younger, and I knew that I wanted to play as much as I could before I hung up my boots. Of course, I was disappointed, but I had total respect for Brian. He had at least been honest with me. Gareth Southgate had already joined from Palace. He had started out as a defensive midfielder, and Brian was looking at dropping Gareth back into the centre of defence, which meant even more competition.

There was no way I was going to stay at Villa Park to sit on the bench, as much as I really didn't want to go. I loved my time at Villa with the lads, staff and fans. I had made my top-flight debut at the age of 27 and more than held my own against some top players. I had a major cup winner's medal and had come close to being a league champion.

I still love the club dearly. In the end Chris Coleman didn't sign for us – he went to Blackburn Rovers instead – but Gareth did make the transition to central defender alongside Ugo and Macca, so my reason for leaving was justified.

Carol and I decided to move into a small village just outside Southport called Tarleton.

Our friends and family would be happy. They could cut down on their petrol costs, at least.

CHAPTER NINE
Tranmere Rovers

THE MOVE TO Tranmere Rovers almost felt like I was going full circle. I had moved away from the northwest some years before, playing non-league and professional football on the south coast. I then moved to the Midlands and hit the jackpot in terms of playing for one of the biggest clubs in the country in the top league in the world, playing in Europe and winning major silverware. At 31, Tranmere felt like the right move for me and for Carol and the kids.

Both our families were delighted with the move – although after agreeing to the deal, it almost broke down because of typical football chairman politics. My agent at that time was a guy called Phil Smith. My dealings with Phil had been minimal during my time at the Villa, as my contract was pretty solid and I was happy with it. But Phil was instrumental in the move to Prenton Park and proved his worth. He had been speaking to Tranmere and, according to Phil, had secured me a better deal, and I was very keen to find out what it was. Good job I was sitting down when he gave me the figures!

I may have been dropping down a league, but in financial terms the deal was a step up. I was to be given a £100,000 signing-on fee per year and paid £2,000-per-week; I was on £1,500-per-week at Villa. I would also become Tranmere's most expensive signing, as they would pay Aston Villa £450,000 for my services. As if all this wasn't enough, I got on really well with John King, Tranmere's manager, and had done so for a number of years. Tranmere had got to three consecutive playoffs and had also taken Villa right to the wire in *that* League Cup semi-final just a year or so before.

So Carol and I were very excited as we made our way to the

boardroom to sign on the dotted line. In the room with me were the manager, John King, the club secretary, Carol, Phil and the chairman, Frank Corfe. Frank had been instrumental in the rise of Tranmere the decade before, alongside Peter Johnson. He had an ego that bore all the hallmarks of what he had achieved. It was all very cordial, and then the chairman decided that he was going to change the deal there and then.

Phil had outlined the terms and straight away Frank bellowed out, "No, no, no. We didn't agree to this."

With this, Phil stood up and looked over at me and Carol and informed us that we were leaving. I looked at Carol and we just got up and walked out with my agent, not saying a word to each other but both of us wondering just what was going on. As soon as we got out of the door, I asked Phil what he was playing at. It was a great deal for me and the family, but it was turning into a disaster. Carol looked worried. Phil pointed to the end of the corridor and reassured us that we wouldn't reach the end of it before we were called back in. Sure enough, the door opened and we were requested to return. In the short time the three of us had been out of the room, the club secretary had told Frank that what Phil had stated was what had been agreed, and the club should not go back on its word.

It was such a relief to us that we had been called back in, and I think it was the quickest contract I ever signed when it was presented to me.

We drove back down to our house in Walmley and started the ball rolling with the sale. Luckily the deal went through quickly, and the next thing we knew, we were living in Southport again. In football life, changes can happen very quickly. Footballers these days have their entourage and a team to do this, but back in 1995, we did it all ourselves.

I joined Tranmere just before the start of the 1995–1996 season, so I only had about a week to train with the team – not long to get to know Johnny King's training regime and my new teammates. I may have been on more money than I had been at Villa, but the difference in the training and other facilities were a world apart. I had loved training at Bodymoor Heath, with its big expansive car park and world-class facilities. At Tranmere, we would drive to an old disused industrial site to get picked up and driven to a local park to train. It was very bizarre to start off with, but I soon got used to it.

My debut for Tranmere came on 12 August 1995, the opening day of the season, in a home match against Wolverhampton Wanderers. The game was an entertaining one which ended 2-2, and I was quite pleased with how I had performed. Our two goal scorers that day were Liam O'Brien and John Aldridge. Both had played in the two legs of the 1994 League Cup semi-final against Villa, and that was a bit of an ice breaker when I was first introduced to the team. It wasn't just Liam and Aldo either, but Eric Nixon had been in goal when I had put that header and penalty past him at Villa Park. Now we were teammates. The same with Alan Mahon, Ged Brannan and a few others. It was all good fun, but it was like facing a pack of hyenas at the time. One would say something and the others would just follow. I would just bide my time and remind them of the winner's medal that I had on the mantelpiece back home and that it was my goal that had wiped out their lead!

There was a lot of pressure on the team due to the past three seasons when Rovers had come so close to making it to the promised land. We were one of the favourites for promotion and one of the teams to beat. We won our next two games after the Wolves draw, against Sheffield United and Huddersfield Town. I actually broke my finger in the Huddersfield game when I went for a challenge in the air and fell on one of their players.

Our first defeat of the season came at Oakwell, the home of Barnsley. We lost 2-1. I played OK, but the injections in my finger hampered me somewhat. Nevertheless, it was a solid start for me and the club. John Aldridge had been on the scoresheet in all four games, and he was as sharp as ever.

As the season progressed, we were looking good for either automatic promotion or the playoffs at least. We suffered the odd loss but had far more wins and draws. I had another hernia in my groin tissue in November 1995. It was exactly the same tear that I'd suffered at Villa. In fact, it was the third time in my career. It couldn't have come at a worse time for me either. It meant that I would be out for six weeks at least, and I would miss most of November and the whole of December, the time when the games come thick and fast and a period that can prove to be decisive in how the rest of the season pans out.

During that period, we won three games on the trot and then inexplicably we lost five consecutive matches. It was so frustrating to be on the sidelines. I just wanted to help the lads get back to the winning ways. We beat Oldham Athletic 2-0 on Boxing Day to stop the rot, but I could tell those defeats were laying heavy on John King's mind. He was under pressure to right the playoff defeats from previous seasons. I was recovering from my hernia injury and was confident that we would soon get back on track.

But that Boxing Day victory was our last one in the league until 3 March 1996, when, funnily enough, we beat Oldham again! I'm sure our fans on the terraces requested that we play them every week!

Frank Corfe and the board viewed our rapid decline with a lot of interest, as the chances of us playing in the Premier League were decreasing match by match. There was talk trickling down that John King's time as manager was coming to an end. Two wins in nearly three months was well short of expectations. I could once again see that it was affecting him a lot, and I really felt for him. He had achieved major success with the club but, ultimately, the board's patience was wearing thin.

The breaking point came after a 6-2 defeat at Derby County on 8 April 1996, a result that put paid to any real hopes of promotion. In fact, it left us perilously closer to the relegation zone. It was an awful run for us.

John was relieved of his duties as manager just four days later, but not from the club, though. Frank Corfe was shrewd enough to know changes needed to be made but that the fans would be in uproar if King was just thrown on the scrapheap, such was his popularity with them. It was announced very quickly that John would move upstairs and become Director of Football.

Stepping into the managerial role was John Aldridge, who became player/manager. Aldo's CV was impressive. He'd won trophies with Oxford United and Liverpool and played in major international tournaments for the Republic of Ireland under big Jack Charlton. Aldo proved to be a popular appointment with the players and fans. By the end of the season, we had managed to get ourselves away from the drop zone, but the big disappointment was not getting anywhere near the playoffs. We finished in 13th place.

My relationship with Aldo when we were teammates was a good one. We weren't bosom buddies, but we got on well. It was also that way at first when he took charge of the team during his first few weeks and months. I think he was finding his feet and evaluating the players and where the team was going. He was waiting to stamp his mark on the team, and that was where things started to go wrong for me at the club and where my relationship with him began to deteriorate. It wasn't anything to do with my playing ability, because I was still in the team and I was still captain.

It's not just football, but in other walks of life there are times when a new person comes in and wants to make their own mark on the situation. John Aldridge was no exception, especially as this was his first foray into management. Looking back, I can fully appreciate why he did what he did. What I can't accept is how he went about it.

If Aldo had pulled me to one side and told me he was looking for new players, that his hands were tied financially and the only way to bring in new signings was to sell those on the biggest contracts, I would have accepted it. Sure, I would have been disappointed, but I would have appreciated where I stood. But this never happened, and I was basically blanked by Aldridge. If I was walking down the corridor and he was coming the other way, he would avoid making eye contact.

I was stripped of the captaincy and in a short space of time I was out of the team, eventually not even making the bench. The players were asking me what was going on and I had no answer for them – because I didn't know myself. I felt like he had made me look like a fool. I would be picked in the squad, and I was made to turn up on match day only to find out that, at best, I would have to sit in the stands. From being captain to that. The approach that Aldridge took was just totally wrong.

I should have known something was up when something happened while I was still in the team. At the time, I couldn't understand what had happened, but it all started to make some sense later on. Aldridge had managed to sign the ex-Wimbledon and Crystal Palace defender Andy Thorn. He was brought in to partner me – or so I thought! I got on with Andy both on and off the pitch. We had played a home game, and I had arranged to meet Carol in the players' lounge afterwards. I went up there to find Carol wasn't there. I asked the bar staff where Carol was and was told that she had left the lounge and said she would wait for me in the car. I found it to be very strange and went out into the players' car park. I asked her what she was doing and couldn't believe what she said.

As agreed, she had been waiting for me in the lounge when Andy Thorn walked in and dropped his trousers right in front of her. When she went to make a complaint, she was told that she had been making false accusations and the powers that be told her to leave immediately. She was told that she would serve a ban until an investigation had taken place. There were other people in the room who had witnessed the incident and not one of them came forward in support. At the time, I couldn't fathom why any of this had taken place. The following Monday I went to see Frank Corfe and he tried to tell me it was all Carol's fault. Frank was even in the room at the time of the incident. I told Frank what I thought of him in no uncertain terms.

But why did Andy do this and why was Carol's word not taken seriously? I don't think I need Columbo for this! Closed case.

I was now training with the youth players and knew something would have to give. After everything the club had done to me since Aldridge had taken over, I still didn't feel inclined to ask for a transfer. Why should I? I had given my all to the club, as I had done with all my previous ones. To have been made captain was an honour. I wasn't going to let them lead me on their merry dance so easily. In the end, the solution was via the loan route, firstly taking me just a couple of miles away and the second one taking me across the world to far-flung places.

Being a footballer was never boring!

CHAPTER TEN
The Loan Ranger

So near: Preston North End.

ALL IN ALL, I played just five times for Preston when I was there on loan. When Tranmere notified me that Preston were looking to take me, I jumped at the chance. I sat down and talked it through with Carol, as I always did, but I knew it was a no-brainer. Preston was just up the road from where we lived and it would take about half an hour to get to training and to the ground, and Carol was more than happy with that. No moving house and I could play football, something I was missing a lot.

Gary Peters was the manager of Preston, and we got on well from the start. All parties knew that it would be just for a month or so, but Gary pointed out that if I liked the club and where it was going, it could be made a permanent move. I went into it with my eyes fully open. I was clearly not wanted at Rovers, so I would give it my all – like I always did – and see how things went.

I was impressed with the changes bring made at Deepdale and could see that the club was looking towards the future. We didn't actually train at Deepdale. This took place at a horticultural centre that also housed football pitches. It was called Myerscough College. I trained with my new teammates for a couple of days at the end of January 1997 and made my debut for the club on 1 February in a home match against Chesterfield. We lost the game 1-0. I was happy with my performance but obviously not with the scoreline.

We made amends with a 1-0 win away at Rotherham in the next game. Another good performance from me and the team, and even after just two games, I felt part of a team unit once again.

A couple of days later and we were heading to the south coast to play Bournemouth. It was the first time I had been back there in a competitive match since leaving in 1991, but it wasn't a good return football-wise, as we lost 2-0. Still, it was nice to be applauded by the home fans before the game. I always got on well with Bournemouth supporters, and the reception I received pleased me a great deal.

It was back to winning ways at Deepdale in my fourth game for the club as we beat Wycombe Wanderers 2-1. My final game for the club came on 22 February when we travelled down to Kenilworth Road and got trounced by Luton Town 5-1. My partner at the back that day was David Moyes, who went on to manage Everton, Manchester United and West Ham United, amongst others. We got run ragged that day. It was just one of those games. They won the second balls in really dangerous areas and made us pay for it.

The following day, I took a call from Gary Peters, who informed me that the club couldn't afford to take me on a more permanent basis. When I'd arrived at Preston, I could see that money had been spent on developing the ground and they had recently purchased Sean Gregan from Darlington for £350,000, so in some ways I was expecting it. He thanked me for my time with the club – as I did him – and expressed disappointment that we could not take it further. And so did I. I still had another week before I was due to report back to Rovers, and Gary told me to take it off and that he wouldn't say anything. I thought that was a nice touch and so did Carol. It meant I could do some of the stuff in the house that I had been promising her I'd do for months!

I never thought for a second that things would have changed at Tranmere during the month I had been away. And I was right. When I returned, I trained with the kids and that was it. Nothing more and nothing less.

A couple of weeks before the end of the season, I received a phone call from Peter Guthrie, an old mate of mine from Weymouth who had gone from there to Spurs. We had a good catch up, and he told me that he was now playing football in Hong Kong at a club called Happy Valley. He asked me if I'd like to go over there and do the same. I had no idea about the playing and wage structure out there, but Peter assured me that as an ex-Premier League footballer, I would be well looked after. Pete passed me over to a guy called Mr Chan (I never knew his first name) and he explained how it all worked. It seemed strange talking money over the phone with a guy I had never met before, but I knew Pete, so it was OK with me.

Mr Chan told me that my Tranmere wages would be matched at the very least and I would go there for three months. I told him I would make a decision within a couple of hours, and I went home to speak with Carol. There was no way I could say yes to that one on my own. We were a family, and Hong Kong is on the other side of the world. Even if it had been next door, it would still have been the same process. We sat down and went through the pros and cons. We figured out that we had not been scared to move to the other side of the country, so it should be the same for the other side of the world. We informed family and friends and they understood. We were a football family and it was part of the job. We were not giving up the house, so they knew we would be back.

There was a lot to sort out, and top of my list was to ask for a meeting with John Aldridge. It was strange to walk into his office, as it had been months since he had last spoken to me, but it had to be done. I told him that I had been given an opportunity to play in Hong Kong. I honestly thought he would jump at the chance to wave me goodbye given our total communication breakdown. But all he did was look at me and say, "What a great move for your career."

He couldn't have been more sanctimonious if he had tried! It really pissed me off. I had an idea come to me and, with no time to think about it, I said, "Anyway, I cannot take the move."

He looked at me and I could see the colour drain from his face. He wanted to think he was in the driving seat whilst putting me down. "Why not?" he asked.

"Happy Valley will only pay half my wages," I said.

His immediate reply was, "We will pay the other half."

Yes, I had been naughty and economical with the truth, but I didn't care. He and the club had treated me badly and this was payback time.

I called Mr Chan back and told him that it was a yes after

just going over the terms once more. He was pleased and said he would call me back shortly with the flight details. I knew I would be going out on my own for a couple of weeks to check things out. I spoke to the FA about it and they were able to advise me.

Within the hour, Mr Chan called me back. "Please start packing and get everything ready for your arrival, Mr Teale," was his opening line. "You have a flight booked from Heathrow Airport in two days."

"Thank you, Mr Chan," I said curtly and with a professional tone. I put the phone down and grabbed my luggage bag from the loft.

The move was on, and new adventures in another country beckoned.

***

So far: Happy Valley.

Two days later, I flew out from Heathrow Airport. Before you ask, no, it wasn't business class. Remember, I was a 1980s and 1990s footballer. The superstars were waiting in the wings to board the money train.

We stopped at Kuala Lumpur, where I was met by Mr Chan and told that I'd get a connection to Penang, where the players were currently training ahead of the new season. In England, football was slowing down for the summer, but in Hong Kong it was ramping up. I would be met at the airport and taken to training camp, where I could start to acclimatise to the conditions and meet my new teammates.

The flight time was only half an hour or so. The heat hit me as soon as I stepped off the plane. We got into a waiting car and half an hour later we were at the hotel. I went to my room, put everything down on the floor and then went down to the foyer, where I was greeted by Peter Guthrie. He looked great, and obviously life out there was agreeing with him. Pete told me that there were a few ex-pats in Hong Kong, which made the move even better. They included Ian Muir, who'd had a great career with Tranmere Rovers (I'm glad someone had), and Martin Kuhl, who had played for Portsmouth and Birmingham City, amongst others. We also had Paul Wood, another ex-Pompey player who'd had a spell with Sheffield United as well.

On the first night, I was put in a room with three of our Chinese players. They were very accommodating and friendly to me, but unfortunately, they didn't speak English and I couldn't speak Chinese. I guess I was feeling a little homesick as well and decided to move my mattress into the room that the other English lads were sharing. Pete was our gang leader and suggested that we go for a little walk. We eventually came across a corner shop, and Pete spoke to the owner, who then proceeded to bring out five chairs. We all sat down and the next thing we knew, the shop owner had come out with some cans of cold beer. It was a process that the shop owner copied on a few more occasions during the evening – so much so that he had five pissed-up English blokes chewing the fat and generally having a good laugh. I liked life over there straight away!

The club authorities knew we would end up having a drink, as this was the British culture at the time. That was in complete contrast to how they really wanted it, though. The next day we were starting a training session. At first it was light, which suited me, as I had only just arrived and needed to get used to the heat, which on that first morning had reached 40°C. Then the training regime stepped up a few notches. I think it was to make a point to the British lads. We were then told we would be partaking in lengthy running sessions. We all looked at each other and the penny dropped.

So we did the session, and I can tell you that it was one of the hardest sessions I have ever had, but we got through it. The next day we had our first proper game, and it was classed as a pre-season friendly. Pete pulled me to one side and told me that the game was all about me and that the club would be watching me at all times during the match. They wanted to make sure I was worth their time and money for the next three months. It was no contest at all, as we won by around six goals. It was an absolute stroll in the park for me. I kept it simple but effective, and I knew I had impressed them. The next day we trained again, and then we boarded a plane to Kuala Lumpur and then on to Hong Kong for the serious business in hand.

The rest of the team went home and me, Paul and Martin

were taken to our hotel, which was on the mainland. It was called the Panda Hotel. There was no way I was ever going to get lost – not surprisingly, it had a drawing of a massive panda on the side of the hotel! It certainly wasn't a tourist place, either. The population was purely Chinese. I could see why they had done it. They wanted us away from any type of drinking culture and for us to integrate ourselves into their culture. They were paying our wages, after all. To get to training we had to take the underground system, called the MTR. It was a very quick way to get from A to B. We couldn't drink, but boy, did we watch some movies. After a week or so, we started to buy all the hooky films that were popular at that time. They were so easy to buy over there. The days would consist of travelling to training, travelling back and then watching films all night. The training was very intense, so watching films was all we wanted to do – it was our way of relaxing. We were able to buy a couple of beers, but that was it. Nothing extreme. The beers were always lovely and cold, which was the complete opposite of the bottles of water we were provided with for training. It was always around the 35°C mark and the bottles were always warm. We would moan about it, but the club didn't take kindly to that, and the request to have colder water fell on deaf ears. The training soon intensified. I could see why some footballers decided to pack it in and move elsewhere, but I wanted to succeed, and it was a challenge I wanted to embrace.

One thing I had not been made aware of was that in this part of the world, every footballer in the league needed to pass a particular fitness test. You would get three attempts and if there was no success at the end, you would be on the next flight home. No wonder they do not tell you these things at the start! We had three weeks to get ready and then players from other clubs, as well as Happy Valley, would participate in the test. It was more about endurance. The actual test consisted of completing seven laps of a 400 m track in 12 minutes. That meant we would have to be pretty damned quick. I wasn't the quickest of players, as everyone knew, but what I lacked in speed, I made up for in tenacity. But let's face it, I didn't need speed to play where I did. Nowadays, the players have fitness sessions based on their positional play. That means that specialists like box-to-box midfielders and wing-backs require speed training, whereas central defenders and goalkeepers have different needs. They have specialised training coaches for each department. Back then we were all bunched together. At Villa, most of the five-mile runs were always led by Yorkie, Earl Barrett, Deano or Froggy (Steve Froggatt). At the back you'd always find me, alongside Bozzie and a few others.

Our first session for the test was just awful. A few of the Chinese lads were doing well, as was Paul Wood, who, in fact, was at the front, but the rest of us failed miserably. Our regime was always the same from that moment on – train for pre-season, train for the fitness test and play in pre-season matches. We did this in Hong Kong and also in China.

It was a wonderful but very strange experience. They put us into a hotel which had a 24-hour golf course attached to it. It was 18 holes and floodlit all the time. It was quite luxurious too. One day we travelled from the hotel to play in a pre-season match. It was miles away and we were travelling on what must have been one of the very first coaches ever made. The seats were ripped, it was rickety and it had no toilet facilities. All the English lads were at the back, and we were voicing our concerns, which, not surprisingly, got us absolutely nowhere. We stopped off for a pre-match meal and we had absolutely no idea what was being brought out for us to eat. We were asking the Chinese lads what was on the plate. They really tried to help us, but there was a language barrier. My palate was all over the place, but I respected that this was the culture we were now living in. Finally, there was a fish dish that came out that was more to our taste, and we got stuck into it. In the meantime, the Chinese lads continued eating whatever was coming out. One dish that made its way over was a plate of beetles – they were lying on the plate with their little legs in the air. The way you were supposed to eat them was to put them in your mouth, spin them around a little, suck the insides and then spit the shells out. There was no way that I was going to try them, but I have to say that after I'd spent some time over there, I did try and eat things that I wouldn't normally consider over here, like snake, which to me tasted a little like chicken.

We got back to Hong Kong after the trip to China and

continued the training, and then we got to the day of the fitness test. The pressure was firmly on, but at least there was the cushion of two strikes before you were out.

I was told that I would know if I had passed the test straight away and then the club would arrange for Carol and the kids to come over to join me. In the meantime I would be shown some apartments. This was the carrot they dangled in front of me!

I passed first time with 12 seconds to spare. Like I had done throughout my career, I simply dug in. It was such a great feeling. Everyone was happy and hugging each other. The language barrier did not matter at that moment in time.

The next morning, Mr Chan came round to congratulate us, and I could tell he was really happy. He told me that the tickets were being sent to Carol. He then took me, Paul and Martin to a place called Lantau Island, a resort called Discovery Bay. We got there by ferry, and it took around half an hour to get there and back from the mainland. It was a mixture of high-rise apartments (although not as high as we have over here) and houses. Whatever we picked would be paid for by the club. It was a beautiful place right by the beaches. It was a very popular place for footballers, and not only for those at Happy Valley. Whilst it was great news that my family were moving in with me, the places were unfurnished, mainly because the place was a popular spot for footballers, which meant that there was a healthy turnaround of players coming and going. I had decided that I would have mine fully furnished, or at least habitable and comfortable, before Carol and the kids got there. There was a plaza right by the ferry terminal, and that was where the players who were leaving the country sold their unwanted furniture, so Martin, Paul and I spent a few nights buying stuff and helping each other move. I had spoken with Carol, and we had agreed that an apartment would be better for us. I can only describe it as something like a Spanish holiday home, with good-sized bedrooms, a lounge and a very small kitchen.

I was made up when Carol and the kids got there. I had them back and I had sorted out a lovely place for us to live in a tight-knit football-dominated community. The only ways to travel when on Discovery Bay were via the bus service or a golf buggy, because there were no cars on the island. I enquired about buying a buggy but decided, after hearing how much they cost, that the buses were a really good alternative method of transport. The buggies were around £350,000 to buy!

The following few weeks were all about training for me, helping Carol and the kids make friends, and settling in and getting the schooling sorted. It had been a great move to Hong Kong, and we intended to make the most of it.

There were just eight teams in the league. The other big teams apart from us were Instant-Dict, Sing Tao and South China. The other thing of note was that there were only two stadiums in Hong Kong. The one on the mainland, called Mongkok, held about 5,000 fans and had no cover – it was a concrete jungle. The other was on Hong Kong island and was the national stadium. This had much better facilities and held about 30,000 fans. There were fast food outlets like McDonalds inside. You can guess which one I preferred to play in! We seemed to play the league games in Mongkok in front of average crowds of around 2,000, and the cup games were played at the national stadium, where the average gates were around 8,000. The results didn't go too badly, and we were very solid in defence. Alongside me was Martin Kuhl, and we had Pete in goal. I liked Martin and we still talk from time to time to catch up. He was a great bloke, but when he stepped onto the pitch, he became a warrior and always looked angry – I would have hated to play against him. It was scary enough being on the same side! After each match, it was the custom for the club to invite the players and their wives to a Chinese banquet. I had started to get used to the food, and Carol was keen to try more as well. It was always in the same restaurant, and whilst the Chinese lads drank water, we got to know the staff, so the English lads were given cold cans of beer. It was only little cans of Heineken, but they were still refreshing. After a while, we'd have so many on the table that we could make pyramids with them. It wasn't that we were pissed up, because they were only small cans, but we got merry. We would take some of them back to Discovery Bay. We'd have a bagful of cans and take them onto the ferry back, having swigs as we went along, and then we would have a few in the plaza.

The club was independent of the famous Happy Valley racecourse, but we had pitches slap bang in the middle of it. We soon found out that there was an English bar right opposite the racecourse, and a lot of the ex-pats who were not involved in the game would go there. We soon became regulars ourselves, so we had a good social life. There was no way we could get absolutely tanked up like we could back home, because it was that hot, the beer just seeped out of you like you were in a sauna!

We found out that there was a small island where they catered more for Western tastes. Whilst I was starting to enjoy the culture, it was great to go over there and eat more familiar food. The players would meet their wives over there, as there were many ferries to and from the island. Our ferry had a bar on it and took a lot longer than the ones the wives caught, so we were well oiled by the time we met up. We did this ritual a couple of times a week but never before match days, when we would all go home and rest up.

Every now and again the club dignitaries would join us at the banquet. We all had to wear the club tracksuits and look the part when that happened. There were always three very important people who turned up, and they always requested that the British lads sat on their tables. On one of those occasions, we were sitting together when the food was brought out. It was soup, and one of the lads did no more than take a spoonful of it and out came a bat on his spoon! We all looked aghast, as his reaction had been picked up by the VIP guests and the clubs' coaches. Peter had been there longer than the rest of us and decided to ask why they had served us bat soup. Peter looked at the rest of us and said, "Come on, lads, we ain't stopping here any longer," and so off we went.

The next morning in training, the coaches didn't acknowledge us and we were singled out for extra training. We were taken down to the beach, which had the softest sand I had ever been on, and they made us run on it for a couple of hours. We were well and truly in the doghouse, but the strangest thing was that afterwards, they took us for breakfast as if nothing had happened.

We had done pretty well in the league and had beaten some of the top teams, but it was their equivalent of the League Cup where we did really well, beating South China in the final. I was happy with the way that I had taken to life and football in Hong Kong, and I was even called up for the national team. Our biggest game was against Iran.

I had come to the end of my three-month loan. It had been a great experience, but Carol and I were now busy arranging to come back to England. We later went out for a meal with Mr Chan. It was a lovely evening, and I brought up the fact that I was heading home soon and had really enjoyed the experience. Mr Chan just looked at me and said, "What do you mean, you are going back home soon?" I thought he was joking and it went quiet for a couple of seconds, but I knew he was deadly serious. I told him that my three months were up. "You can't go, you can't go," was the reply from Mr Chan. He was visibly upset and made his excuses and left. Carol and I just looked at each other – it was all very strange. However, we didn't hear anything else after that and made our way back home a few days later, although we hadn't had time to take the furniture down to the plaza to sell on. The lads left over there sorted that for us.

It had not been more than 10 minutes since I walked through the door of our family home in Southport when the phone rang. It was from a Mr Lam, who was one of the club's owners. He told me that he was going to sue me for every penny I had, as I had broken my contract for the year. A year? I told him that he was mistaken and that it was for three months, and I needed to report back to my parent club, Tranmere. He insisted that the contract was for a year, not three months. I told him to check with the English FA, as they would confirm what I had told him. I put the phone down, looked at Carol and told her what Mr Lam had said. She was none too happy with the news, but we carried on unpacking.

Shortly afterwards, I received another call from Mr Lam. He could not apologise enough, as he had received confirmation that I was right after all – not that I had any doubts. However, he asked me if I would come back. I told him that I would have to speak to Tranmere first and I would get back to him. Tranmere wouldn't pay half my wages, as they had done before, but they were happy to let me go. I then told Mr Lam that I would come back for another nine months and he promised he would make it worth my while. So two days later I was back on the plane going out to Hong Kong again, and Carol and the boys joined me again not long afterwards.

The dust had not settled on our old apartment, and the club

paid for us to live there again. Mr Lam ensured that the kids received the best schooling, and I was paid more money as well, so it was a no-brainer. Ryan excelled in the school he was at, but Nathan less so. He was a more hands-on type of lad and not as academic as Ryan. We agreed that he could return to England and go to his previous school, with Carol's sister looking after him. Remember, we'd only gone out there for nine months – it wasn't permanent, and we wanted the boys to be happy.

The lads were really happy to see me again and I was back in the team straight away. It was really surreal going back, and we spent the New Year in Bali being treated like kings and queens. The league closed down over the New Year period, and the four of us (Nathan had come back to join us for the Christmas period) hopped onto the plane on New Year's Eve and made the New Year celebrations with just minutes to spare. We found a bar that was full of Australians who just wanted to party. It was a great night, and the kids played on the beach right in front of us. We went to bed and then woke up on 1 January 1998 to cracking hangovers.

The very next day saw Bali fall into a total financial collapse. I was not aware of just how bad the crash was until I went to the bank to change £100 and left with loads of notes in a carrier bag. It only needed the words SWAG on the bag and for me to wear the eye mask and it looked like I had stolen it! By the way, with that £100 we were able to dine out at the finest restaurants and we booked into a top hotel – we had the best of everything. By the time we flew back to Hong Kong, I worked out that all those fine things we had experienced had only cost me £50! It really is penthouse and pavement in Bali, and we got talking to some of the workers on the beaches. We would buy trinkets we didn't need just to help them out. One of the workers told Carol that she needed to start selling tights, as they were hard to get hold of and she could make some money. Carol took her details and promised that she would help out if she could. When we got home, one of the first things she did was buy a box of stockings and send them to the worker's address. A week or so later, Carol received a letter from the lady, who said she had been bowled over by her kindness. I was so proud of Carol, and I still am.

We got back into the serious business of playing football, and we finished runners-up, so it had been a very successful season for Happy Valley. Soon afterwards, I was called into the office and told that my contract would not be extended. Whilst I was disappointed, I could see it coming. They had paid me far more than any other player, especially when I had returned for the extra nine months. It had been a truly wonderful experience that we as a family would never forget. We had last one trip to Australia, as Ryan had already been booked on a school trip, so we flew over there while he was on his educational trip and saw the sites down under. Flying in from Hong Kong meant it was nowhere near as time-consuming or as costly as it would have been to travel from England.

We said our goodbyes to the friends we had made and took the furniture down to the plaza for some other footballer to use.

On the way home, we flew to Dubai and decided to stop there for a couple of days. Dubai was nothing like it is now, and we stopped in a hotel where the pool was on the roof and the sun looked massive in the sky above us.

We had travelled about a bit, but now it was time to come home. As we hit the runway at Heathrow on a cold day in May, about to catch the train back to Southport and home, it dawned on me that I was now without a club for the first time in my career. It was a daunting thought and stayed with me until we got home. Seeing Nathan again was just the tonic I and the rest of the family needed. We were back together again and I was happy. Maybe it was time for me to look at new horizons job-wise.

I was a painter and decorator by trade, and I thought about starting my own business. That was my final thought as we tucked the boys into bed as our first day back in Southport was coming to an end. I kissed Carol goodnight and turned the light off and went to sleep.

However, the next morning when I woke up, all I could think about was playing football. It wasn't quite time for me to hang up my boots after all. But where would I be playing? I would never have guessed the destination in a million years, but soon we would be off again. This time to another country, although one where we wouldn't need our passports.

CHAPTER ELEVEN
Motherwell

BRIAN MCCLAIR HAD been a pivotal player for Manchester United in the early 1990s when United, and Alex Ferguson's rise to greatness, began. I'd had some great tussles with him in Villa's games against the Red Devils when we were title contenders. He was an intelligent player who put himself about, whether that was up front or later, in midfield. He had returned to Motherwell, the club that had given him a start in the game, in the summer of 1998. Interestingly, Choccy, as he was known, was part of Aston Villa's youth set-up in the early 1980s.

One of the first things he did on his return to Scotland was help Motherwell find seasoned pros who could help the club. Choccy had found a list of players who were available on free transfers. He saw my name on the list and told the club to get in touch.

A few weeks after returning from our adventures in Hong Kong, our next-door neighbour, a lovely woman called Rosemary, asked me to stain some new wooden windows for her. I told her that it would be no problem. So, one morning, I was up a ladder staining the windows when the phone rang at home. Carol answered it and on the other end was a guy called Willie McLean from Motherwell Football Club asking to speak with me. Carol took his number and promised him I would call him back later in the day. It turned out that Willie was the brother of Tommy McLean, who had played for Rangers and a few other clubs north of the border as well as representing Scotland. Tommy was the Dundee United manager at the time.

I finished staining the windows and called Willie back. He informed me that Choccy had put my name forward and asked if I was interested in having a trial with the possibility of signing for the club if all went well. I was 34 by this time and it seemed like a good challenge. I spoke to Carol and the boys and they were keen to try living in a different country and gaining a new experience.

Just a few days later we had packed the car and were heading up for pastures new north of the border. The club put us up in a lovely hotel in Hamilton. I wasn't keen on having a trial, but I understood where Motherwell were coming from, because they wanted to check out my fitness. We played the French club Le Havre in my trial match. I cannot remember the score, but I knew I'd given a good account of myself, and this was confirmed when Motherwell told me that they wanted me to sign a two-year contract. I would be made captain and would be expected to help the youngsters coming through the ranks. I was given a £5,000 signing-on fee and £1,500-per-week. The manager at the time was Harri Kampman, who was a lovely guy from Finland. I got on him with straight away.

Motherwell had some good pros in their ranks like the goalie, Stevie Woods, defenders such as Eddie May, and Billy Davies in midfield. We got down to some serious pre-season training. The younger lads were a cocky bunch, but it honestly didn't bother me – I had been the same at their age, to be fair, and I liked that attitude. It used to rile Billy Davies, though. The future Derby County and Nottingham Forest boss often told me to "put them in their place". Billy was a fiery character to have around and was always moaning that he wasn't getting the chances he wanted. His glass was certainly half empty most of the time. Another reason why I didn't mind the youngsters' attitudes was that as I was barking out orders and telling them where to go, they were doing all the running for me. It's fair to say that running was not my favourite part of the job. Put me right in the middle, going for a 50/50 ball or up for corners and I was your man, though.

It was one of the younger lads who scored the winning goal on the first day of the season, my debut. We beat St Johnstone 1-0, with Jed Sterling scoring the only goal. I found out early doors that whilst football in Scotland was technically not as good as south of the border, it was still a very tough league to play in; no one gave you a quarter.

Our next game was away at Rangers, and the difference in

attendance epitomised the difference between the two Glasgow clubs and the rest of the clubs in Scotland. Against St Johnstone there had been just shy of 6,000 fans in the ground. When we played Rangers, the crowd was nearly 50,000. Having smaller crowds has its advantages when you are playing well. It's almost like having a one-to-one conversation, as it brings you closer to the fans. The other side of the coin is that when you are not playing so well, you can hear every single word they say. Having come from non-league, I knew you needed to develop a thick skin to play in those environments. At 34, mine was rhino-like. We actually played well at Ibrox that night, and we only lost to a last-minute penalty. Owen Coyle was our main 'Johnny on the spot' that night, and in truth, he was most games. He was a good man too.

We'd made a solid start to the campaign but then went on a losing streak. The first loss in that run was a 3-0 defeat at Hearts. I always found Tynecastle a hard place to go. The vast majority of football stadiums that I played in during my career seemed to have stands that slowly rose up from the pitch, but it was not the case at Hearts. It just seemed to come out of the ground at a very straight angle, and it could be quite daunting just looking at it. Add in a fanatical support base and the fact that I was English, it really made for a red-hot time.

The wind of change was soon blowing over Motherwell. Firstly, in the boardroom, with John Boyle taking over from the Chapman family. John had made his name in the business world with Direct Holidays. There were also changes in the management hot seat as well. Harri Kampman was a lovely man, but right from the get-go, I had a feeling that he was a little out of his depth managing the club. After four straight losses, Harri resigned, but we all knew he'd been pushed.

A few weeks before he left, Harri took us to play a friendly against Utrecht in the Netherlands during the international break. We were staying in Amsterdam, and we had been told in no uncertain terms that we could not go out and break curfew. That lasted all of one second, and soon us older lads were leading the rest of the boys into the city centre. I became the 'Bank of Amsterdam' that evening, as I was lending money to the players who wanted to engage with some of the workers in the city – and I'm not talking those working at the Van Gogh Museum!

It was a total shock to me when Billy Davies was given the manager's job. Not because I didn't get on with him, but he hadn't been playing and, if you remember, his glass was always half empty. Billy was quick to bring in some new players like Ged Brannan and Tony Thomas, who I had played with at Tranmere. John Spencer and Don Goodman also came in. Billy called a meeting. It all went well and he still kept me as captain.

The rot stopped with a 1-0 home victory against Rangers, with John Spencer scoring the only goal of the game. The place was rocking in the stands, on the pitch and in the dressing room after. A few games later we were playing at Kilmarnock. I went up for a challenge and split open the gash in my head that had been caused when I had played for the Villa at Swindon a few seasons earlier. But a few stitches and I was right as rain. We had a decent run under Billy and then got thrashed at home 7-1 by Celtic. Henrik Laarson bagged four goals in that match, and he nutmegged me for one of them! After the game we all had a beer to drown our sorrows. I gulped mine down and just wanted to get home to Carol and the boys. As I walked into the car park, a taxi driver came speeding up and missed me by inches. He pulled up and let's just say he threw expletives at me in relation to whether I had parents and also voiced his dislike of the country I had been born in. The poor taxi driver failed to put his window up, and I grabbed him around his throat while he was sitting in the car. He deserved it for the abuse he had given me. Doing it on the pitch was one thing, but not off it!

We kind of made amends a few weeks later with possibly our best result of the season when we beat Dundee United away 3-0.

By that time, Andy Goram had joined us in goal. I loved Andy's character and personality. I always loved it when we played Celtic, because Andy was a Rangers boy and he loved winding up the Celtic faithful. Andy was a great keeper and he was a few years older than me. We were both nicknamed the Grandads. "Piss off, you cheeky buggers," we would shout, but we knew it was all good banter.

You will recall that I told you that the players didn't give you a quarter in this league, and once again, I was in the wars in a home match against Hearts on 24 April 1999 – a game we lost 4-0. During the match, I was elbowed in the face by a young midfielder they had, called Scott Severin. It was just one of those things, but once again the blood flowed. In the hit parade of injuries that I had had in my career, this was number one.

I suffered a depressed cheekbone, a broken jaw and damage around my eye. I had to have a metal plate inserted into my face. I gave the following interview to the *Scottish Sun*.

> I'm not ashamed to admit that I ended up in tears. The pain was so intense I was almost up the wall. I've had four hernia ops, broken my nose twice and snapped my medial ligament, but Saturday's agony was by far the worst. All I remember is jumping for the ball and the next thing being hit by an elbow or a head. I feel that something's run over the side of my head.

Needless to say, my participation on the pitch finished earlier than I had expected it to.

We finished the season in seventh place and overall, I had really enjoyed my first full season in Scotland.

After the season, Billy Davies called me on my mobile while I was shopping for a new camcorder for a family trip to the United States, and he told me that he had been very pleased with my contributions and that there would be a new contract waiting to be discussed when we came back from the summer break. I told Carol and she was made up. I had family in America, so the family spent a good month or so over there in the close season. The kids loved it on Redondo Beach in California.

We came back for pre-season training, and we got into it straight away and looked forward to a new season. I concentrated on my fitness and put any contract talks to the back of my mind. Billy didn't mention it, and I put that down to him getting prepared for the new campaign. We started the season in pretty much the same vein as we had the previous one. We drew a couple and won and lost in the same measures. I managed to score two penalties in consecutive matches to keep up my perfect record taking spot kicks. We lost 6-5 in a crazy game at home to Aberdeen and then beat Dundee United 2-0 at Tannadice. I scored the second goal from the spot. I actually missed it first time, but the referee ordered a retake, as the keeper was well off his line. I made no mistake with the second attempt.

During this period, I was wondering what was going on with the new contract talks. Billy still hadn't said a word, and one day during training, I asked Pat Nevin about it. Pat was still playing football at the time but was also part of the management set-up, although in what capacity, no one was sure. Pat told me that it was being looked at but said, "Let's wait a few more weeks and then discuss it properly." I found that a little strange but just got on with it. A few weeks later, I brought it up again and was told to "give it another few weeks". At that point, I started to smell a rat. I hadn't asked for this new contract, Billy had come to me about it, and I felt that the club should at least discuss it with me as they had said they would. Another couple of weeks passed and there were more fob-offs. I really wasn't happy with the way that the club was acting over this.

At the start of January 2000, we had gone away for a mid-season break. The Scottish press had come out with us, and you would get players and staff speaking to them at various points because we had a good relationship with them. At the end of the break, I was contacted by one of the press guys asking if I had seen one of the national papers. I really cannot remember which paper it was, but it was all about my contract situation. I had not uttered a word about this to the press and was shocked to read, "If the big man thinks he is getting what he wants, then he can think again." The quote was from Billy Davies and the big man in question was me! I couldn't believe what I was reading. The red mist descended, and I decided that I needed to set the record straight. Remember that no details had been discussed at that time. The only thing Billy had mentioned was "We are looking to give you a new contract, Shaun!"

I called a journalist I knew at the *Daily Record*, a guy called Derek McGregor. He was a good hack and I felt that I could trust him. We are still friends to this day. He had started his career at the *Bournemouth Echo* when I was playing at Bournemouth, and we had got on really well. Trust was very important to me. Derek listened intently as I explained what had actually happened – that the club had instigated the new contract talks, but they kept putting it off when I brought the subject up. I was upset that Billy had told the press that no way would the club meet my demands. What demands? It hadn't even got that far. I felt like I was being treated like a piece of meat, and that was the overriding theme of the article that Derek wrote for the paper. I discussed how unhappy I was with the board, Billy and Pat. The article came out and the following day, I was summoned into the manager's office to discuss things with Billy. I had originally walked into the club to put my training kit on, but it wasn't there, and that was when the kit man, Johnny Hardy, told me that I was expected upstairs.

I expected the chairman to be there, but it was just Billy and one of his assistants. The first thing Billy did when I walked into the room was to throw the *Daily Record* at me, and to my surprise, I actually caught it and threw it back at him. I had a smile on my face at that point, but it wasn't throwing the paper that caused it. The table in the boardroom was very high. Now, Billy isn't the tallest person in the world, and all I could see was his head just above the table – and that was what made me smile.

Billy demanded to know why I had given the interview. Was he playing me? I couldn't believe he was asking me that when *he* had been the one who gave the original interview stating that I wouldn't be getting what I wanted. I reminded him again that it was *him* who had brought up new contract talks with me in the first instance and that was as far as we'd got. I told him that he and Pat Nevin had been stringing me along and I was not having it anymore. He told me that the chairman wasn't happy with my article and that he was fining me two weeks' wages and suspending me. I laughed in Billy's face and gently reminded him that it would have to be one or the other, as that was the law. I could see he was losing face a little. He told me to leave straight away, that I would still be paid but the suspension would stand. With that, I walked out of the office and never played for the club again.

It was such a shame that it came to that after the first 12 months at the club. The Scottish PFA got involved to see if they could broker peace talks, but it had got to the point where it was going to be really difficult to do so. My contact at the PFA was Gordon Smith. He played for the likes of Brighton and Rangers and was making a name for himself at the PFA since he'd stopped playing. He was a very good footballer in his time, but he will always be remembered for missing a golden chance for Brighton in the 1983 FA Cup final against Manchester United. There were only minutes left and the game was locked at 2-2. There is a famous commentary from the BBC, "And Smith must score . . ." He didn't, and the match went to a replay, where United won 4-0. I got to know him very well during our dealings and I liked him a lot. I got a call from him out of the blue one day to say that a club from Sweden was interested in signing me, and he asked if I would go for a trial. The usual rules applied, so I spoke to Carol, and we agreed to go over there. The team in question was called IFK Norrköping, and they played in the top league in the country.

We flew from Glasgow Airport. If we thought it was cold in Scotland, we were in for a mighty shock when we landed in Sweden. It was −11°C and it hit us straight away. We were picked up by the club's driver and we made our way to Norrköping. The roads were thick with ice, but the driver was so used to the conditions that he was going fast and driving like it was the middle of summer. It was pretty scary, but he knew what he was doing – I think! We met the some of the club's directors in a coffee house to discuss what would happen next. We were informed that they had sorted out a hotel for us. We got into the hotel's reception and booked into our room. Upon booking in, we noticed a lack of people around. It was very quiet. In fact, it was too quiet for my liking, and then we found out the reason why. The hotel had over 200 rooms and we were the only ones staying in it – the rest were closed! We were taken to our room and once the door was shut, we all fell about laughing. It was so surreal. I kept on shouting out, "Here's Johnny," like the Jack Nicholson character in the film *The Shining*. Every time we left the room, we half expected to see those eerie twin sisters from the movie!

We went to look around the town and it was just stunning, but it was getting colder, and the ground was now very thick with ice. I was told that I would be picked up for training at 6 p.m. Luckily the training was going to be in a gym, which I discovered when we got to the ground – or so I thought! We changed into the kit provided and I said hello to some of the players in the changing room. That was when we were told that the gym was actually five miles away and we would be running there. It felt like Hong Kong again, but without the gloriously hot weather. A few minutes later and I was running in a pack with a few of the players, and I didn't have a clue where I was going. As you know by now, running wasn't my favourite part of being a professional footballer, and I had to keep up with the leaders of the pack so I knew where I was going. We got to the gym and I was blowing out of my backside. We were given a football and played it around and then the coaches started to put out loads of cones. It basically meant that we would have to do 16 running exercises. Now, you can imagine that after the run to the gym, I was really looking forward to that! We had to complete it with pace, and to top things off, there were no windows to open or air conditioning. We had to do this set *four* times, and I can honestly say that no football match I had ever played in previously made me feel so tired. However, we did it, kicked a few more balls about, and then we were told that the session was coming to an end. All we had to do was run the five miles back to get changed! This was turning into a nightmare of epic proportions. We ran back to the ground, where we showered and got changed. I was told to report to the head coach. I was thanked for coming over and told that I had done well. However, the club weren't going to sign me, because they thought I was too small to be a centre half.

"Too small?" I said, shocked.

I asked the coach to repeat the reason again and he obliged. I just sat there in total disbelief. I had played in England for 20-odd years and I had played for some of the biggest names in the game. At no stage was my height discussed with any of them. And here I was in Sweden being told that this was why they weren't signing me. I just wanted to get out of the place, but I kept my dignity and asked them to take me back to the hotel to make arrangements for our return to Scotland. Carol couldn't believe it when I got back and told her what had happened. After a few minutes, she said, "Good job. I never liked the place anyhow. It's too bloody cold."

With that, we packed and left the Overlook Hotel (it wasn't really called that, but if you have seen *The Shining*, you will understand) and caught the next flight back to Scotland. As we landed, my phone began to ring. It was Tony Thomas, who I had played with at Tranmere and Motherwell. He told me that a friend of his was at Carlisle United and wanted to sign me. They would pay me exactly what I was earning at Motherwell. Life and football are so strange at times. I got on the plane from Sweden thinking that I hadn't got a club and would be stuck out in the wilderness at Motherwell and was being offered the chance to play for another club by the time I stepped off it.

As soon as I could, I called Tony's friend Martin Wilkinson, who was the manager of Carlisle United. Martin told me that there would be no trial; they really wanted me, and not just for what I could offer on the pitch. He said nothing more, and I discussed it with Carol and she said, "Well, we'd better go and check out this Carlisle place, then."

I looked at her and smiled.

My football career in the UK had taken me from the northwest of England to the south coast, the Midlands, back to the northwest and then north of the border to Scotland.

Now it was taking me to just south of the Scottish border.

Have boots, will travel, as they say!

CHAPTER TWELVE
Carlisle United and Finding My Way Back Home

WE TOOK A look at Cumbria, although we didn't move up there when I played for Carlisle United. It was only an hour from our house in Motherwell, so it made sense for Carol and the kids to stay there while I trained and played.

Martin was true to his word. I had no trial and I signed in February 2000 until the end of the season. He told me that my first game would be an away trip to Plymouth Argyle, and what a journey that was – over six hours on a coach each way and a round trip of some 780 miles! There were a few pit stops on Friday 4 February 2000 as we travelled down for the game the following day. It sure was a long journey, but it did mean I could get to know the players better, so it wasn't all that bad. We lost the game 2-0, but we couldn't blame the long journey, as the team had been in around the bottom of Division Three for most of the season. There was real danger of us dropping out of the league.

Carlisle had escaped the drop the year before on the very last day of the season when Jimmy Glass, a goalkeeper who was on loan at Carlisle, came up for a last-minute corner and scored the goal to keep United up. I was informed that if we stayed up and I played my part, I would be offered a new contract with something different attached to it. I was turning 37, and I had a strong feeling that something different would be a role in a managerial capacity of sorts. This was something that greatly appealed to me, so I knuckled down to play my part.

Our first win came at home against Barnet on 18 March. We won 3-1, with Stevie Halliday scoring a brace. I had played with

Stevie at Motherwell, so I knew he was a good striker. What he lacked in height, he made up for in skill, and he was able to twist and turn the opposition defences. We also shared driving duties, as we lived close to each other in Motherwell. There was a third person in the equation as well, as Rob McKinnon joined our driving club too. I had talked Rob into coming to play with us. We were still in a very precarious position, but we managed two wins on the trot for the very first time in the season when we came away from Peterborough United with a 2-0 victory.

During the next 10 games, we picked up two further wins against Swansea City at home 2-1 and Chester City away 1-0. The Chester game was crucial, as we were 23rd and they were 24th, so these three points were absolutely priceless. They threw everything at us, but we scored a last-minute goal through Rob Dobie, and it was such a relief when he scored. We were all tub-thumping in the dressing room afterwards, believing that the result would be enough to keep us in the league – not that we were counting our chickens, because there were still six games to go.

Our final game of the season was on 6 May 2000, and it saw us once again travelling down to the south coast, with the club's coach driver clocking up even more mileage. Despite our valiant efforts at the Withdean Stadium, home of Brighton, we lost the game 1-0. It was nerve-racking as we waited for the Chester City result to come in. One of us would be playing non-league football come the end of the day.

In the end, it was a massive relief, as Chester lost 1-0 to Peterborough, so we avoided relegation on goal difference – two goals better off than Chester City.

We had only just avoided the drop, but at least we had done it. I was pleased that the club would be talking to me about the new contract they had agreed if we retained our status as a professional club. A couple of days later, I received a call from the club asking me to meet with the chairman, Michael Knighton, the man who had famously tried to purchase Manchester United in the late 1980s.

Knighton was an extrovert (aren't most people in his position who own football clubs?). He had walked onto the pitch at Old Trafford during talks with the United board and done keepieuppies in front of the Stretford End. The deal did not come off, and several years later, he purchased Carlisle United instead.

Michael informed me that Martin Wilkinson was stepping away from his managerial duties and they wanted me to take over. I was made up. This was the step up that I wanted to take, and now I was being afforded the opportunity. Michael informed me that he would set up a meeting with the rest of the board with a view to making it official. Carol was very happy when I got home that night. Arrangements were made for me to meet up with the board a couple of days later. I told Carol that I thought the meeting could become protracted and I may have to be in Carlisle for some time. She suggested we get a hotel for a week or so, and that is what we did. We booked the Holiday Inn in Carlisle. One of the other guests staying there at the same time was the comedian Roy 'Chubby' Brown. He was a lovely guy, nothing like his on-stage persona. He came and talked to the kids at breakfast time, which was a really nice touch.

It was time for the board meeting, and the feeling that I had about talks being protracted became reality. I was there for hours as the board diligently went through each player and what they brought (or didn't) to the club. Basically, it was a 'should he stay or should he go' scenario. After the meeting, I was told that the board would have a further meeting to go through my responses and then they would get back to me. I informed them that we had booked our usual family summer holiday and I was assured that we would pick it up again when I came back. I cannot remember where we went on holiday, but I can certainly remember a week or so later when Carol picked up an English newspaper with a headline saying that Carlisle United had appointed Ian Atkins as their new manager! We just looked at each other and couldn't speak at first until it sunk in. Two things shook me.

One, me not getting the job, and secondly, Ian Atkins was a staunch Blue Nose (Birmingham City player and supporter).

We had a few days left of the holiday, but the news had thrown me. I was asking myself, *Where does this leave me?*

On returning from the holiday, I called the club. At first, no one could tell me what was going on. Or maybe they didn't want to? I finally got through to one of the directors. Initially I was told that after careful consideration, the board had opted for Ian Atkins. In fairness, I understood the decision. The club had to make the decision that was best for them, and while I may not have liked it, I had to respect it. In turn, I asked the director why respect wasn't a two-way thing. Could the club not have informed me as a matter of courtesy so I wouldn't have found out about it in one of the national newspapers? I wasn't going to win that one, so I politely stated that I should at least be honoured with the new contract that I had been promised if we stayed in the league. The director called me back a few hours later and said that the club would offer me a three-month contract on a third of my current salary. I didn't have to mull this over for too long and told them to stick the offer where the sun don't shine.

I had worked out that Atkins didn't want another senior player around – someone who wasn't afraid to tell it like it was – and therefore I got the derisory offer knowing I would refuse it.

Tough decisions needed to be made, and we agreed that as there was no chance of getting back into the Motherwell set-up, we would sell our house up there. We still had our house in Southport, so we knew that was where we would go, and then we would see how the land lay.

In the end we sold the house in Motherwell to Jock Brown within the space of a week. Jock was a lovely man who had been manager of Scotland. While we were packing up, I got a call from Barry Hedley, who was one of the directors at Southport. He had read the papers and knew what had gone on north of the border and asked me if I would consider playing for Southport again. I told him that I would, and we arranged to meet the following week.

Mark Wright had taken over as Southport manager – the very same Mark Wright who I had admired at Italia '90; the man who had been a great servant for Derby County and Liverpool. The very same guy I had sat in front of as a Villa player when I was suspended watching from the stands at Tranmere Rovers in 1994 when he had wished me luck against Manchester United in the final.

Carol and I had talked about moving back home a few weeks before we'd sold up. Now I had received a call from the club asking if I would go back. The planets aligned, I guess.

Southport seemed like a magnet to us.

We were homeward bound once more.

I stayed at the club where it had all started for one more season. It was a bit of a strange start for me, even though I knew I would be playing, because Mark had brought in a couple of young players who played at centre half.

I played more of a sweeper role for the first six games. It took a bit of time to get used to it, but my age and experience meant that I was prime for it. The trouble was that I played the first six games and was then named on the bench for the following six before being picked again for the six after. It was a really strange set-up. Halfway through the season, Mark Wright was sacked by the club. Not so much for the football side, but he was alleged to have made remarks about Mavis, the chairman's wife. I am not sure about the finer details, but the chairman will always win if there is a dispute.

The club then made Phil Wilson the manager. Phil, or Pancho as he was known, had been around the non-league scene for what seemed like an eternity. He knew the ropes. He had also been around sunbeds by the look of it, as he was always tanned, regardless of which of the four seasons we were in.

I got on well with Phil and his team. We didn't pull up any trees, but we were solid. We managed to win our last game of the season and, as is the case in non-league, it's in the dressing room, after the final game, where the manager outlines his vision for the following season and whether you'll be part of it. I've mentioned before that non-league football could be brutal. For some reason, Phil didn't outline next season's vision, so we all just went home. His assistant told us that he wouldn't come into the dressing room, and we would hear from him in a week or so. I sat there and thought about what had happened at other clubs, with false promises and changes made by previous managers. At times, us players are treated like cattle. I wanted to change that, and the only way was to get into management myself. I would have to go out there and hustle, rather than wait for it to come to me. I didn't want any player under my watch to have to go through what I had been through. I decided I would continue to play, but with the caveat that it came with a management role.

So imagine my surprise when the very next day, I took a call from a guy called Frank Parr at Burscough Football Club. Frank told me that the club was interested in me coming in as player/manager. Frank seemed like a really good bloke, but I had to be blunt with him. I asked for assurances that if I came to see him and he liked what he saw and heard (and vice versa), then we could sign the contract pretty sharpish. Frank agreed that this could happen, so we had our meeting, both liked what we saw and heard – and the contract was drawn and signed pretty sharpish.

I was now a player/manager for the first time in my career. And it felt great.

CHAPTER THIRTEEN
I'm the Boss!

THERE COMES A time in every footballer's career when we know when it's time to retire from playing. Then we have to decide if we want to stay in the game in some capacity or indeed get out completely. There are some players who don't even like the game; they have just been given the talent to play it – and pick up the paycheque at the end of the week. I would say that in my experience, the vast majority of players love playing the game, and I am definitely in that category. I still believed I had a couple of years left as a player but certainly wanted to explore the managerial side, so the call from Frank Parr was fate. Pure and simple.

The contract formalities were done very quickly, and then it was down to working out what I wanted to do for the impending 2002–2003 season. There wasn't much to sort out family-wise, because Burscough was very close to Southport, and we were able to stay at our home, the Winning Post.

The first thing I did was sort out an assistant for myself. I wanted someone I could completely trust – someone who would not be afraid to challenge my decisions, not sulk if I disagreed with them, and also be bold enough to put forward ideas of their own. That person was Ray Stafford. I had known Ray for a number of years, and I knew that he was taking his coaching badges. He fitted the criteria well, and I knew he would be great around the players. Ray was very much a people person who knew how to pick the lads up when needed, and I was really pleased when he accepted the job.

We quickly arranged the pre-season friendlies, so they were set in stone. Burscough had a good set of players, but both Ray and I knew that we lacked experience in certain departments, so we held open trials over a couple of weeks. Our mantra was if you think you are good enough, then come along and let's see if you can come on our journey. That philosophy worked really well for us, and we were able to pick up some very useful acquisitions. We had a goalkeeper called Matty Taylor, and his brother came to one of these trials. His name was Joe and he was well over six foot. Ray and I discussed his merits and decided that he could play with me at the back. We also looked at the non-league free transfer list, and we found four very good players that fitted our ambitions for the club. We picked out four or five lads and they were given contracts as senior pros. Those guys included Carl MacAuley, who had played for Liverpool in his youth. He was a very experienced right back in non-league terms and he slotted nicely into the right back berth. We already had our left back, Ryan Bowen, who had been at Burscough for several seasons. So the backbone of our defence was something I was looking forward to developing. We also brought in a number 10 called John Norman. He had played against *the* non-league team at the time, Yeovil Town, in the previous season's FA Trophy. He was a very clever player who was hard to pick up and played in the hole. He created goals and scored them too. Up front we brought in Gary Martindale. He had played for Bolton Wanderers and knew the leagues well. We also brought in a guy called Paul Burns who had only recently retired from the game. He was a small in stature, but I strongly felt that he still had something to give and could feed off Gary well. Luckily, we managed to change Paul's mind, and he became an important part of the set-up.

I was happy with the squad and how we had gone about things in the summer. One of the pre-season friendlies was at home against Preston North End, and I was looking forward to that one. Even though I had only played at Preston for a month, I'd enjoyed my time there, so it was good to see the team come and play at our place. What made this even spicier was the fact that good old Billy Davies was now their manager. It was quite clear that the bad feeling between us after what had happened at Motherwell were still festering, not so much from me but from Billy. He decided that shaking my hand and looking me in the eye were off limits for the duration of the time that his club was being entertained by mine. Fortunately, I didn't lose too much sleep over it, just in case you were worried for me.

The season started and things got serious. We weren't at the top of the league but at the same time not really bothering the bottom half either. Ray and I had a really good system going, with me on the pitch and him in the dugout. I could control what was going on where the opposition were attacking, and Ray could do the same when we were on the attack. It was one of those years in the league when we didn't pull up any trees, although we were solid throughout. However, we excelled in the FA Trophy, and by the end of the campaign, we had written ourselves into cup folklore.

Just before the first round, Frank informed me that the club finances were not looking as healthy as they should have. He told me that we needed to cut back on players' wages, those who were on contracts with us, and I just shook my head at Frank. This brought back all sorts of memories from my playing days when I'd felt that the players were being treated unfairly and like cattle. I had come into management not only to test myself but to shield the players from that sort of thing. I immediately called a meeting with the players and told them that under no circumstances should they accept any type of pay cut. I knew that that wouldn't be favourable with Frank and the board, but I felt that this was the right thing to do for the players. Either that or the players would be entitled to leave the club on a free transfer. I was just starting to build a good solid base and didn't really want either solution.

It was shortly after this that we started our run in the FA Trophy. I knew we'd receive more money for every round we progressed. The more money that came in, the less likely it would be that Frank and the board would approach the players about pay cuts.

The first round saw us drawn at home to Marine, a local team that played in Liverpool. It was a very boring goalless draw with both defences coming out on top. A couple of days later, we took the short trip to Merseyside for the replay, and we came away with a 3-1 victory. It was just as dour as the first match, but we got through, although one of our goals was a very fortuitous one – the kind that is very lucky but also a sign that a team can go all the way.

Frank was happy because it meant we could pay the players, so it was all good all round.

We were then drawn away in the second round to Harrogate Town. We found ourselves two down and looking like we would be exiting the cup far too early, but Joe Taylor pulled a goal back before we were awarded a penalty, and can you guess who took it? Yes, yours truly. And my 100% penalty record remained intact. We won the replay 3-2, which meant that we were through to the third round, which is when the big guns from the Conference enter the competition.

There was no need for a replay in the third round, though, as we won 3-0 at Ilkeston Town. The fourth round saw us once more play away, this time at Alfreton Town. That too went to another replay that was held just a few days later. We won that one 2-0. It was at this point that we knew the club finances were OK, but we also knew we had a shot at actually winning the cup. It was the same feeling that I had experienced in 1994 with the Villa after we'd beaten Sunderland 4-1 away in the third round. Sunderland had chance after chance and we had just four and scored all of them.

There was also a buzz around the club which had not been there in the previous rounds. We were now into the last 16, but a few of the big guns were still in it. We wanted a home tie and we got it when we entertained Wakefield and Emley, who were in our league – the Northern Premier League. Cup fever had caught on in the town. Our normal crowds were around 200, but for that tie there were 437 in attendance. It was a real spectacle for them, as we destroyed Wakefield and Emley from the get-go. It was a surprising result, as the league games against them had been tough with very little between us, but in the cup, we ended up winning 5-0.

So sixteen teams became eight, and one of them was Yeovil Town, managed by Gary Johnson. They were coasting the Conference League and were the holders of the FA Trophy too. They were the last team we wanted to be drawn against, and definitely not at their place.

The draw was made and . . .

Yeovil Town were drawn to play Burscough at home! The one thing we didn't want was that, and we were a little disheartened. We soon got over it, though, and made sure we maintained our concentration going into the game. Before the game, absolutely no one gave us a chance. The bookies had us at very long odds, whilst Yeovil's odds were small. This was a real 'David and Goliath' match, as we walked out to almost 5,000 fans. There were probably a couple hundred of our fans, but boy, did they make some noise. Our game plan was to nullify their attack, because they were dangerous on the flanks. Ray and I had gone to see Yeovil play, so we were able to determine what we needed to do. We needed to play a deeper game than we were used to playing, and it worked a treat. They couldn't get behind us. We scored our first goal midway through the first half through Peter Wright, the man I'd had brought in from Preston North End. At half-time, I told the lads to do exactly the same for the second half. Peter Wright took it to heart, and thankfully we were two up a few minutes after the break. We were in dreamland and managed to hold out. In fact, we had a chance to make it three, but it wasn't to be. I guess I just had to be satisfied with a 2-0 victory away to the biggest and best club in non-league football!

The result shocked the non-league football world, and we started to receive plaudits for what we had achieved. I have to say that Yeovil were absolute class after the game. Gary Johnson came into our dressing room to congratulate us, and he brought the FA Trophy in so we could take a look at it and see what we might actually win. It was a wonderful moment, as was the journey back up north, as we sang, drank and had a bloody good time.

The semi-final saw us paired with Aylesbury United, with the first leg away. The other semi-final was Tamworth versus Havant and Waterlooville. The first legs were played on Saturday 5 April 2003. Our game finished 1-1, with their goal scored by Craig Maskell, who had previously played for Southampton. Craig had played in Hong Kong for Happy Valley as well. That was on my recommendation, even though I hardly knew him personally. Things didn't work out for him over there and he was soon back in Blighty. I was a bit surprised that he didn't want to speak to me before or after the game. The only thing I could think of was that he blamed me for what had happened over there, which seemed very unfair. Seven minutes after his goal, we were all square when Gary Martindale equalised. It was a game we should have won, in fairness, but at least we were very much in the game when we locked horns a week later. It was very much nip-and-tuck, with neither team giving too much away. Then, with just minutes to go, we were awarded a penalty when Peter Wright was brought down in the box. It was a blatant penalty, but the Aylesbury players protested – protested and protested. I picked the ball up and just walked around the pitch until the referee finally blew for the spot kick to be taken. I walked up to take the penalty spot as always, decided where I was going to hit it (this time down the middle) and didn't look at the keeper. I hit the ball and it went exactly where I wanted it to go. The referee allowed Aylesbury to kick off and then blew the final whistle. We were in the final, which, ironically, was being held at Villa Park. Our opponents in the final would be Tamworth, who had knocked out Havant and Waterlooville by the aggregate score of 2-1. I couldn't ask for anything better, could I? The football gods were smiling down on me.

After the semi-final win, I went to sit in my little office and let the lads enjoy this moment on their own; they had earned it and made me proud of what they had achieved.

We had a few league games to play before the final, and I twisted my ankle in one game, so I decided that I wouldn't play in the last few league games so I could be fresh for the final. I wrapped myself up in cotton wool and did the usual things a manager has to do. I travelled down to Lancaster Gate and had my photo taken with the trophy, as did former Nottingham Forest player Gary Mills, who was the gaffer at Tamworth. His side were clear favourites to lift the trophy, which suited us down to the ground, as we wanted to be the underdogs.

Steve Walsh was Tamworth's main defender. He had played a pivotal role in the rise of Leicester City in the 1990s. I knew him well, and we later had football adventures of our own across the pond.

You will have to keep on reading to find out more!

Playing against a very good Leicester City team in the 1995-1996 season. This is me going for the ball against Lee Philpott. Just look at the concentration on our faces!

Playing for Happy Valley in Hong Kong was a great experience.

I had some great tussles with Mark Viduka during my time in Scotland. He was a beast of a player and hard as nails on the pitch. Just the way I liked it!

SMASHED FACE LEFT ME IN TEARS

By ALAN NIXON

MOTHERWELL hardman Shaun Teale has revealed he was reduced to TEARS by the sickening injury that has ended his season.

Teale suffered a depressed cheekbone, broken jaw and damage around his eye in an aerial clash with Hearts youngster Scott Severin on Saturday.

The Fir Park skipper had a metal plate inserted in his face in an op last night, and won't play again for more than two months.

Teale winced as he recalled the horror moment. He said: "I'm not ashamed to admit I ended up in tears.

"The pain was so intense I was almost up the wall. I've had four hernia ops, broken my nose twice and snapped my medial ligament, but Saturday's agony was by far the worst.

"All I remember is jumping for the ball and the next thing being hit by an elbow or a head. I feel as though something's run over the side of my head."

Meanwhile, Spurs are lining up an ambitious scheme to make Well their nursery club.

Secret talks have already taken place between Well and the London giants to try and forge a link.

The idea is the brainchild of Tottenham's Director of Football and former

The only time I ever cried because of a football injury.

Enjoying my last days as a professional footballer with Carlisle United. What a blast it was!

Coming full circle. I rejoined Southport in 2000, the club where it all began.

Getting my foot on the ball in the final of the FA Trophy. Such an honour to be playing and managing the team on that very special day.

So very proud of my team. No one expected Burscough to win the FA Trophy, but we proved them all wrong.

Winning the League Cup with Villa was so very special, and lifting the FA Trophy with the team that I was managing at Villa Park was written in the stars for me. A perfect day.

Still working hard at 42 as manager of Chorley.

With my grandson Ellis at a Preston v Aston Villa match.

My family, my world. With Carol, Leyla Jane, Ellis, Ryan, Riley Joseph, Arrabella, Thiea Rose and Nathan.

I also gave a number of press interviews, and one of my favourites was with *Preston Today*:

Teale calls for the spirit of Yeovil tie.

Burscough boss Shaun Teale wants his players to recall one match before Sunday's FA Trophy final against Tamworth – the 2-0 victory that knocked out holders Yeovil Town.

The Linnets' quarter-final victory at Huish Park was the biggest shock of the season in non-league football and Teale believes it can be the inspiration that spurs his side on at Villa Park. "The Yeovil game will be part of my team-talk," said the 39-year-old defender, who is returning to the hometown of Aston Villa, the club he served for four seasons in the Premier League.

"No one thought we would win at Yeovil, and it was something that no conference team managed in the past year," he added. "But we gave a tremendous performance that day and now I want the players to do the same on Sunday. Tamworth are firm favourites with the bookies and that suits us. They are expected to complete a double having won the Dr Martens League. The pressure is on them, not us and we will be determined to do the same job that we did at Yeovil. It is a fantastic achievement to have reached the final. Now having got there, we want to go and win it."

Teale knew his side were bound for Villa Park when they were awarded a last-minute penalty against Aylesbury in their semi-final second leg. A foul on striker Peter Wright allowed the Player/Manager to complete a *Roy of the Rovers* story by scoring the winner, the 1-0 win securing a 2-1 victory on aggregate.

It was soon time to plan how we would get to Birmingham and where we would stay before the final. I invited Frank Parr and the club secretary, Stan Strickland, to the Winning Post to discuss. Frank and Stan allowed me to lead on the subject, as they had never been to a final before and knew that I had been. I told them that I wanted the players to get a really good feeling for their surroundings and wanted them to be able to relax before the game. I suggested that to do that, we travel down on the Thursday. This was the same experience I'd had with Villa. It worked for us then and I saw no reason why it wouldn't now. I said that I would talk to Aston Villa to see if we could use Bodymoor Heath for training. Frank and Stan agreed, so I called Villa to get it all arranged.

The hotel that we stayed at was the Post House in Great Barr, the same hotel where I had stayed when I'd initially signed for the Villa. The club were great as always, and they ensured the players and officials could have a tour of the Villa Park stadium and get a really good feeling for the ground. I was happy with the pre-match arrangements, and the only thing to sort out was what we would actually do if we won the trophy. I didn't want the lads to have to rush back; I wanted them to be able to savour the moment. I informed Frank and Stan that I'd like us to spend an extra night at the Post House with the wives and girlfriends. Their reaction was not a positive one, and the reason was the cost. I suggested that we invite fans to come with us and charge them £10 for entry into the after party. In fact, that was a pretty good idea if we won or lost; besides, we had all been in it together. That way, our rooms would be paid for and everyone could have a great time being together. It was at this point that Frank and Stan finally agreed, but something in me made me think that they weren't really 100% on board.

I would soon find out that my hunch was correct.

The tour of Villa Park was a great one, and afterwards Doug Ellis invited me and Ray into his office. Doug was on form and did his usual conversation pieces, including the story where he reckoned he invented the bicycle kick. I'd heard them all before and took it with the usual pinch of salt. Ray just sat there open-mouthed and was like a sponge, just soaking it all up. It was a funny sight, I have to admit.

The team I picked for the FA Trophy final at Villa Park on Sunday 18 May 2003 was:

Goalkeeper: Matty Taylor.
Defence: Shaun Teale, Joe Taylor, Carl MacCauley, John Lawless,
Midfield: Ryan Bowen, Peter Wright, John Norman, Gary Martindale,
Attack: Mark Byrne, Paul Burns.
Subs: ***John Bluck, Chris McHale, Gary Maguire, Marvin Molineux, Michael White.***

We all relaxed on the morning of the match, and Ray and I reminded the players that we were there to play the game, not the occasion. The crowd was just shy of 15,000, with half of them making the journey from our little village.

We won the game 2-1, and if I am really honest, it was comfortable. Tamworth lost both strikers during the match, but that doesn't really tell the story. Our lads were just better than them on the day, and even if Scott Rickards and Mark Sale had stayed on, I don't think they'd have got the better of us. Both the goals we scored were almost at the same time as those we'd scored against Yeovil in the quarter final. Gary Martindale scored them both. Mark Cooper pulled a goal back for Tamworth with 10 minutes to go, but we held on. I knew my boys would do it, and as the final whistle went, I hugged and thanked each and every one of them. I wasn't being overconfident, but I knew we would win it because we had the eye of the tiger before the game had even started. When it kicked off, we played with smiles on our faces.

We lifted the trophy and then we started the celebrations with the fans. I could not have been prouder. This victory was up there with the 1994 League Cup final win, and I said that to the TV and the other reporters. We got back into the dressing room and gave speeches to each other, and I told them just how proud I was of them. We then showered and made our way to the function room that Villa had provided for us. However, that was where it all started to go horribly wrong, and the plans for the celebrations at the Post House Hotel went firmly out of the window.

To this day, I am not sure why.

I am the first to admit that I'm a vocal person and footballer. I always did it for the good of the team. We had just won the FA

Trophy, becoming the smallest team to do so. We had knocked out Yeovil and beaten Tamworth in the final, and on both occasions, we were serious underdogs.

That in itself should have been the springboard for us to push on.

Anyway, I made my way into the function room and the first person I made eye contact with was Carol. She had a face like thunder and I knew something was up. She needed cheering up, and I noticed the trophy was on Stan Strickland's table. I went over and told him that I was taking it over to our table. I sat down and asked Carol what was up, thinking that me bringing the trophy over would make her happy. It didn't have much of an impact, so I again asked her what the matter was. She told me that it had been a brilliant day but since coming into the function room, some of the Burscough hierarchy had been making the win about themselves, not me and the players. She had taken umbrage with it, knowing how hard we had all worked for it. Villa had been good enough to provide us with the room to celebrate and they were making a lot of unnecessary noise that wasn't just about celebration. I found it all a little disrespectful. I told her not to worry about it, and we continued to have a nice drink and talk with the players and their partners. A little later, I went over to Stan's table to discuss the plans for that evening's activities. I was then told that we wouldn't be going back to the hotel. The coach was outside and would take us all straight back to Burscough. I immediately told him that I wasn't going to do that and neither were the players. Not only that, but I had also booked hotel rooms for some of my mates to join us as well. Very soon after that conversation, the coach was full and ready to take everyone back to Burscough. The board had instructed the players to board the coach. The only representative of the club left at Villa Park was me. It felt very embarrassing to see that happen in front of all the Villa delegates.

Luckily, I had driven down to allow space for others to travel, and it meant I could also go and see my ex-Villa colleagues if I wanted to. The activities in the function room ended abruptly, and Carol and I finished the night at the hotel.

It wasn't what we had hoped for, but we still enjoyed ourselves nonetheless.

The next morning, we travelled back up to Burscough. There was an official party on the Monday, which we all attended. The atmosphere with Frank and Stan was a little strange, but we all got on with it. The whole village seemed to be out in force, so there were plenty of other people to talk to. The management of the club, Carol and I were then invited back to the Lord Mayor's office, and that was when I knew there was a serious issue. Not one of the committee members spoke to us – not even when we had the official photos taken – so after about an hour, we left to have a drink at home.

The next few weeks passed by and there was an uncomfortable silence in and around the club as Ray and I focused on what we needed to do for the upcoming season. It was then time for our family holiday to recharge the old batteries. Before I left, I gave an interview with the local Burscough newspaper, and I was asked about my plans for next season. We were a little club that had achieved big things, but the downside of that was that the bigger clubs would come and sound out some of our players, as is always the case in football. I stated to the paper that we needed to be careful we didn't put ourselves in that position by tying those players who were instrumental to the continued success and progression of the club down to new contracts. I was also aware that the players themselves would now have greater ambitions, so it was going to be a fine balancing act.

Not surprisingly, Frank and Stan did not like my interview and called Ray and me into a meeting. I reinforced everything I'd said in the interview, because in my opinion it was all true. It got a bit heated at the time, but by the end of the meeting we all agreed to disagree and try to move forward.

That was obviously just a smokescreen, and it presented them with an opportunity to discuss a severance package with me. A few days later, I was once again called into the office and told that I was being relieved of my duties, as they didn't agree with my vision for the club. I had just led them to their greatest triumph and because I had been direct, with the fall-out of that, I was no longer welcome to manage the club! I was pretty sure they didn't have a clue about the playing side, so I just exploded and told them what I thought about them and the decision they had made.

They should have been backing me, not sacking me!

They had not expected the success we had given them, and perhaps they thought I felt I was bigger than the club – that was never my intention. I just wanted to progress the team, but at the same time I knew our star players would want to progress themselves at other clubs at some stage.

That was exactly what happened soon after I left the club.

Mike Marsh, who had played for Liverpool, came in to replace me. I heard that he tried to impose his way of doing things (totally understandable), but some of the players, like Ryan Bowen, questioned the changes so soon after we had found success.

They wanted evolution and not revolution.

My first season as a player/manager had ended on a sour note, but overall, it had been a wonderful experience. We had been on a long journey that was full of twists and turns, battling the giants of non-league who were trying to stop us. We knocked them all down.

I didn't know where the new road would lead me, but I knew that I would continue to walk it playing and managing.

As it turned out, I would tread a familiar path.

I started off managing my local village team for around five months while waiting for a suitable job to come along. The team was called Tarleton Corinthians. I didn't get paid, but I loved it nonetheless. They played in the Preston League, and what made it special was that our Ryan played in the team, so it was a real father and son bonding moment. It was a great time too, as we went on to win the league. Funnily enough, it was one of the best times I have ever had in the game. After the season finished, it was time to get back into being paid for managing a team.

I had a few offers, and I started to weigh up my options and take a serious look around. Then I received a call from Dave Stone, the chairman of Northwich Victoria. Dave informed me that the club was in the process of relieving the current incumbent of his duties and asked if I would be interested in taking over. I had a real soft spot for the club, as I'd played centre back for the first time while I was there, and we had also achieved the great escape in the short time that I played for them, so the move to manage the club was appealing to me. Dave asked if I could take training and look at the set-up. Again, it appealed to me greatly. "When are you looking to get me over there, Dave?" I asked, expecting it to be in the next few days.

"Can you come over tonight, please, Shaun?" was the reply.

Talk about being put on the spot. I didn't feel that comfortable with it at first due to the fact that they hadn't discussed the situation with the current manager, a guy called Alvin McDonald. I was assured that it would be done straight away and would be resolved by the time I got there. I told Dave that as long as that was the case and I was notified straight away, I would come over.

Everyone knows football is a dog-eat-dog world, but there also has to be honour among thieves. I was given confirmation that Alvin had been notified, and a couple of hours later, I was leading the training. I had Ray with me once more. The club wasn't doing well at all and were in and around the bottom of the table, just as they had been when I went there as a player, so it seemed that nothing much had changed.

Ray and I took the session with the players and then headed back into the dressing room. Shortly afterwards, Dave Stone came in and introduced me to the lads as "the new caretaker manager". I immediately shot a look at Ray but decided not to say anything. At no point had we discussed this being a caretaker role. Afterwards, Ray and I were driving away from the session, and we decided that whatever it was, we would take it on. We basically had the rest of the season to keep them up, and we saw it as a challenge we were prepared to take on.

The club was being run very badly and no one seemed to have any idea how to put it right. As befits some clubs, the powers that be simply did not want to put their own collateral into the club. That was certainly the case with Northwich Victoria at that time. The club didn't even have its own ground; we shared with Witton Albion. I felt that Ray and I were doing the job with both hands tied behind our backs. I hadn't been happy with being told that it was a caretaker role, but after a while, I was glad it had become that way. It was never going to be a permanent role from my point of view, but I wanted them to stay up at the very least.

I picked myself in six games but soon decided that I would be able to give my best standing on the touchline, because old

Father Time was holding my number up. In the end we just couldn't save them from the drop, and Northwich were relegated from the Conference.

A major impact was the financial issues that the club had faced, but they returned the following year and also had a money-spinning FA Cup tie with Sunderland. I was pleased for the players that I knew there and the fans.

My next management role would turn out to be my last, and it was at Chorley FC. They were a team that played in the Northern League Division One. They were a solid team in the league even if they did generally finish in the bottom half. They were owned by Trevor Hemmings, who also owned Preston North End and a string of successful racehorses, including three Grand National winners. The club had a little money to spend on the back of Trevor's successes – not an amazing amount compared to the higher echelons of the Football League, but very good for where the club was at that time.

We were a good team in the division; one who never bothered the high-flyers but didn't associate with the low ones either. Unfortunately, Trevor withdrew funds at the tail end of my tenure, which lasted 18 months. I think he wanted to concentrate his financial efforts on other areas such as the property market. He also owned Pontins, the holiday camps, so he had plenty to be getting on with.

We had to sell some of our top earners at the club, and as a result I had to step back in as a player, and we had to play some of the players from our junior section. That could only take us so far, and I saw the writing on the wall.

Another thing was that I found I wasn't enjoying it as much as I should have been. Football had been my life. I had taken rejection after rejection to finally get where I wanted to be, and I had loved every single minute while I was a player. Had it been the same as a manager for me? A resounding yes when it came to the vast majority of the players I had in my teams, but working with people in boardrooms who had no idea about the game and were not really prepared to invest in it whilst promising the earth – that definitely wasn't my favourite part.

My last game in charge of Chorley was away at Clitheroe. We lost 3-0. I played out of necessity, and it was during that time on the pitch that I decided enough was enough. I looked around at the players and decided there and then that I was out of there. The club was so skint that it was actively seeking fund-raising initiatives just to pay the players. It wasn't right at all. When I informed the club straight after the match, I was told not to make any rash decisions, but my mind was already made up. I called all the players and staff into the dressing room, as well as some of the suits from the boardroom, and I told them my news. The players looked at each other and I got the feeling that some of them were not surprised at all. I wished them all the very best and shook hands with everyone in the room. As I walked out of the dressing room, it dawned on me that I was leaving football for the first time since I had left school. That was the hardest part.

I will always love the game and have absolutely no regrets from my career, but as for now, well, time to settle the bar bill.

I could seek solace in the fact that I had a profession to fall back on with regards to the painting and decorating.

We'd also bought a pub by then, so there was no way I could take a back seat. It was quite the opposite, in fact. It was time for others to settle their bar bills at our place.

A brand-new career was dawning.

CHAPTER FOURTEEN
Vodka, Cokes and Brushstrokes

WHEN I WAS growing up in Southport in the late 1960s and early 1970s and getting deeper and deeper into football, I would read all the magazines about the game that were in the local newsagents. I read them all back to front and from front to back again. It fascinated me to see so many footballers go into the pub trade after they had hung up their boots. And then there were people like Francis Lee, who played for Derby County, Manchester City and England, doing something completely different. Franny made his money from toilet paper! Some, like Mick Channon, went into horse racing, and others opened shops.

When I played for Aston Villa, one of the most popular sports shops in Birmingham was named Harry Parkes, after the former footballer. Harry had played his entire career at the Villa and was on Birmingham City's board in later life. His sports shop in the city centre was the one that most people went to.

In the main, it was the pub trade that a lot of ex-players went into. Today's players are multi-millionaires who do not have to seek employment when they pack it in, but my generation would, by and large, have to keep working, and I was no different.

The pub that Carol and I invested in was called the Farmers Arms in Burscough.

This is how the *Lancashire Telegraph* reported on the news that I was moving away from football:

Chorley boss Teale quits
By Mike Dawber

Officials and fans of UniBond League club Chorley were

stunned last night when player-manager Shaun Teale resigned because of the "pressure of business." Teale said he could no longer combine the dual role of running the Farmers Arms pub and restaurant in Burscough with his managerial duties at Victory Park.

In the absence of Chairman Ken Wright, who is indisposed, Brian Pilkington, Chorley's acting Chairman made the following statement: "Mr Shaun Teale, Chorley Football Club manager, has offered his resignation and we have accepted it. Shaun informed the club that he has been finding it increasingly difficult to run his pub/restaurant and carry out his duties as manager of Chorley FC.

We understand that Shaun's livelihood must come first, and we wish him well. We appreciate everything that Shaun has done for the club, playing and managing in extremely difficult times for Chorley FC.

Assistant-manager Ray Stafford has agreed to take charge of the team for the weekend matches against Shepshed Dynamo and Ossett Albion."

Teale, 42, who took over the Farmers Arms in Burscough during the summer, said, "I am sorry to leave, but I have my livelihood to consider and I have found that I can't carry on doing both jobs. There aren't enough hours in the day and I felt that if I carried on much longer my health would have been affected. I have done my best on a tight budget to bring success to Chorley. I carried on playing to help ease the club's financial burden, but long hours at the pub and time taken up playing, training and managing the football club have made it impossible for me to keep up both jobs."

Teale's departure came after the Magpies lost 3-0 at Clitheroe, their second defeat in three days. "I would have had to make the choice even if we had won the two opening matches," he said. "There is a good squad of players at Chorley and I wish the club every success."

The Farmers Arms was a lovely place. We often took the kids there for Sunday lunch or a weekday bite to eat, and we started to get friendly with the landlord and the staff. One day, while having our lunch there, we were told by a friend that the pub was up for sale and we should look into buying it. At the time, that was the furthest thing from our minds, but Carol could see that the wheels were turning in my head as we sat down for lunch.

We finished up, drove home and discussed the possibility between ourselves and the boys, who were now well into their teen years. We all agreed that it would be a good move for us and that we would all chip in and make this a family-run business.

Running a pub or bar is hard work, I can tell you – possibly the hardest job I have ever had. It was very long hours, but it could also be rewarding at the same time. A typical day for me started like this:

Up at 6 a.m. to let the cleaners in. We would then get the bar areas ready and make sure the chefs had everything they needed. If not, there would be a trip to the cash and carry. We always made sure that the barrels and kegs were full and the pipes cleaned, and then it was time to open the doors. Eat, sleep and repeat!

I really enjoyed working behind the bar serving our customers. We all had our own shift patterns and it worked really well. We had a lot of Everton and Liverpool fans come into the pub, and there was always great banter with them. We had a lot of repeat custom, which was great for the family, as it showed us that we were doing something right, offering great food and drinks, and that our hospitality was of a good standard. The first 18 months went really well for us and then we hit the financial crash in 2008 and 2009. It seemed to be a worldwide one, and it caused banks to collapse. It massively hit our takings, and here's a good example of how. Pre-financial crash on a Sunday, we were taking around 250 orders for food, and after it hit, we were down to fewer than 70 covers. We had a 72-seat restaurant, and once people had to tighten their money belts, it very quickly looked deserted. We had put a considerable amount of money into the place, and even though we had taken to it well, there was only so much time that we could afford to take a hit before we started to look at bankruptcy procedures.

So we made the decision to sell up.

It was always going to be a hard process in itself, as at that time there was around 40 similar pubs going out of business in the area. Initially we put a price on the place that was realistic considering what we had paid for it, but by the time we eventually got a serious buyer, it had decreased considerably – and we were not alone.

As I've said before, generally the punters were brilliant, but there were times when we had to deal with some awkward situations. The pub was just over the road from a trading estate and there were a lot of similar firms that traded against each other, so there was a little rivalry at times. We would host things such as the Christmas parties for them, and one time it kicked off in the car park. It was like the Wild West without the gunslingers!

I had followed in the footsteps of the 1960s and 1970s footballers that I had grown up watching and admiring, and we had, by and large, really enjoyed the experience. I had tried something new, and it had worked out until something happened that was out of our control. It was a great experience and we had no regrets at all.

So it was back to a profession that I had been in all my life during my non-league days and even kept my hand in when I turned pro. It's par for the course to have a second job in non-league football, as I have discussed previously, and mine was painting and decorating.

The reason that I got into the trade was that when I was younger, my mum and dad had bought some holiday apartments in Southport. I would go and watch my dad put the wallpaper up or paint some doors, and after that, he would teach me the basics and I started to do some of my own. I felt I was pretty good at it, and I would then get asked to do some decorating for family and friends in the area. It wasn't until I moved to Weymouth that it really took off. I was asked what my profession was and I told them that it was painting and decorating. That information was used in the next matchday programme. Within days, I received a call from an ex-player called Gary Borthwick who was also a painter and decorator. He had been a very popular player and had built up a great reputation in the town. Gary asked if I would like to join him, so I did. We got on very well professionally and personally, and we were kept busy. One of our first jobs was to decorate council houses and flats, because Gary had acquired the contract. On the way to one job, he asked me how many rolls I could put up per day. I didn't really have a clue, so I just said I could do around eight a day – it was just a number that I plucked out of the air. I must have impressed him, as we got to the first house and he helped me in with the gear and then he went off and left me on my own to complete all the rolls I'd said I would! All eight of them! I worked really hard to get them done and was pleased with myself when Gary nodded in appreciation.

I never bragged to him again, though!

We worked together solidly while I was playing at Weymouth. I never really lost the skill, and I still did some on the side when I turned pro, just to keep in with it, knowing that I could go back to it after I finished with the game.

And I am still working in the trade today, so it wasn't lost at all.

It's not all about just painting and decorating nowadays, and over the years I have learned to diversify the business. This means that I have learned to fit doors, windows and fascia boards. I still offer all these services, but the main thing that we do now is garage conversions. They are great to get involved in, as it gives me the opportunity to design them as well. I am very lucky that I have built a solid name for myself in the Tarleton and Southport areas, and it gives me enormous pride when I drive past a job that I have completed. Not everyone knows what I did in a previous career, and I find this quite helpful at times, as I can get on with the job at hand and not have to talk about my football career.

The only giveaway is that I wear shorts in all weathers. I'm always asked if I'm cold, and then I tell my client that I used to wear them all the time when I was a footballer. They then ask who I played for, and when I tell them about working for the likes of Harry Redknapp, Ron Atkinson and John Aldridge, they look at me in amazement. Then I find that when I've gone for the day, they end up putting my name into Google and finding out more about me. The next day when I return, they are like the Oracle.

In fact, they often know more about my career than I do!

I sometimes ask them about something to remind me. It's all part of the job. I love it really and wouldn't have it any other way.

So, now you know about the jobs I did, and still do, outside the game.

Now it's time to dip back into football and tell you about an aspect of the game that I was also involved in. Something I have not really discussed thus far.

It all happened across the pond in the good old US of A!

CHAPTER FIFTEEN
Coaching in America

EVERY TIME I made a move in football, it was always by a phone call made to me or vice versa, whether it be as a player or a manager. Now, for actually coaching children, it would be via the power of social media, and in particular, Facebook.

I made friends with a guy called Carl Hedley on Facebook. I knew Carl through his father, Barry, who was one of the directors at Southport. It was good to see him on social media after a few years. Carl messaged me to tell me that he was looking for coaches to run sessions at football camps for a couple of weeks in the United States, where he now lived. He told me Carol could also come over. I would do one week for him and then another similar session at another camp. They would pay for the flights and accommodation for a month and a car, so it meant we could have a couple of weeks' holiday thrown in as well. Carol said yes straight away (why wouldn't she?), so we were soon on the plane to Atlanta, Georgia.

Before the flight to Atlanta, I spoke to a guy called Drew Prentice, who was actually in charge of the camps, just to get more information about them. Drew informed me that he was looking to call the sessions 'the Premier Camp'. His rationale was that he knew I had played in the Premier League and wanted to make a big thing of it. He asked me if I knew any other ex-Premier League players who would be interested in coming over. I'd got to know Steve Walsh very well over the years. Walshy had been the Leicester City captain under Martin O'Neill, and he had also been player/coach of Tamworth when my Burscough team had won the FA Trophy. I thought he would be a good match. So I called him, and he agreed to come over with us. We were provided with a two-bedroomed apartment with a swimming pool, no less. Walshy had one of the rooms and Carol and I had the other. While we were working, Carol would use the pool and prepare food for us.

The camps were very well set up, and as well as Walshy and me, there were two players from the United States ladies' team there too. The second camp was run by a guy called Rob Manjino. I wanted for nothing while I was there. On one of the nights, Rob and Drew came over to our apartment for drinks and food and I was asked if I wanted to take a more permanent role. Walshy had already made his way back home because of the other commitments that he had, but we all had a chat with Carol, and we decided that it would be a good move for us. It was a great place to live, the club was well run, and it gave us a chance to sample life in yet another country and experience a different culture.

We formally agreed the contract and then made our way back to the UK to sort out our new visas. The process was a little cumbersome for the O-1 visas, as it took months for them to come through. It's a specialist visa for entertainers and athletes. As soon as we received them, it meant we would have the visas for three years without having to reapply.

During the time we were waiting for them to come through, Carl Hedley and Drew Prentice had flown over to the UK for a couple of weeks, and I managed to set up a meeting for them with Tom Fox, who was the CEO at Aston Villa at the time. The plan was to tie in the coaching with the club with a view to bringing players over who were good enough to play for Villa. The meeting went very well, but unfortunately, Tom left Villa soon afterwards and the project was shelved.

But when the visas arrived, it was time for us to pack our bags and fly back over to Atlanta for a new chapter.

As it was a permanent arrangement, rather than for just a couple of weeks, we had to sort out our own place to live in Atlanta. We found somewhere not too far from the apartment we had previously stayed in, so we already knew the area. Then, for me, it was down to work. The money I was earning wasn't spectacular in any shape or form, but the experience I would gain was far greater. That was made all the better when Drew informed me that I could also set up my own little academy where I could provide one-to-one sessions.

I went ahead and got it set up and charged the parents $35 per session. I would do this around the group sessions and it worked really well. The club I was working for was called Dacula Revolution. I kept thinking about vampires when I first heard the name of the team, but that soon wore off, much to the relief of Carol and the boys. I was given two teams to run: the under 10s and the under 15s. The under 15s had a reputation that preceded them; they were by and large an unruly bunch, to say the least. I wasn't having any of that. I had come from the brutal world of non-league football, where discipline was king. However, I must admit that I never saw the unruly side of them at all, and they took to my methods very quickly.

Things were working out very well. My business built up very quickly, and I think what helped was that I had played football at the highest level. The American parents loved that. During the second year, I also coached at the local summer camp that we had originally come over for. Walshy was back out there, and this time he brought with him two of his former Leicester teammates, Muzzy Izzet and Steve Guppy, both fine footballers as well as top people and coaches. We also had Ray Hall, who I had worked with when I had been an apprentice at Everton back in the day.

There are a lot of tournaments in America, and I was pleased that the under 15s won the first one we competed in. I was really proud of them. There was an awful lot of admin to complete as a coach in America, as we were required to write reports on each player. With running the under 10s and the under 15s, you can imagine how much time I spent doing those reports. There were four teams in the under 10s! I found some of the rules over there a little strange at times. One of my players got sent off for the most ridiculous of reasons during the second season. We were actually going for the league, and it was crunch time; the last game of the season against one of our biggest rivals. The player in question went to volley the ball during the game, completely missed hit the ball and it ended up hitting his own hand. It was classic ball to hand that would not even be looked at over here. But the referee determined it as handball and sent the lad off. If that wasn't enough for the red mist to descend, the fact that a sending off meant we lost three points was the absolute tipping point. I was furious and told the referee what I thought. I had to be held back. It still makes me mad thinking about that today.

I had a number of run-ins with the officials before that event, and over time I learned to bite my lip, but on the final day of the season, I couldn't hold it in anymore. It wasn't just me, but people who helped run the club also got involved, and it nearly turned into a mass brawl. Not surprisingly, I was reported by the referee for my conduct and the club didn't take kindly to it. I was basically in the club's bad books, and Drew made it very clear that I was out of order. I think that incident and the fact that Dacula Revolution were currently being amalgamated with another club, Gwinnett Soccer Academy (GSA), meant there were no further contract extensions coming my way. There had been talk that I'd be given an extension, but it soon became very apparent that GSA had a host of their own coaches that they were keen to use. Eventually the club paid my contract and it was time to return to the UK.

It was probably a good thing we returned to the UK, because we were looking at getting back to our family and friends in any case. Carol was missing the grandchildren by the time we entered our third season in Atlanta. It was all a little strange the way we left, but there were no regrets. The United States had been a wonderful experience for me and the family. We often think that we would like to get back out there at some point in the future and for me to take up another coaching role, but since COVID, the process is a lot harder and the Americans are now taking on home-grown talent, which shows how far the game has developed over there. Now Americans are coming to ply their trade over here.

We loved the United States and the opportunities that came up at the time. I also did other work for a short while with other teams involving high school teams, both boys and girls.

It wasn't just coaching I got involved in, but also managing the teams as well, so it was basically a win–win situation. I had a fantastic relationship with the players and parents, and it was something that will stay in my heart forever. Our holidays took us all over the States, but our favourite was over in Florida, in Fort Myers. Atlanta could be pretty cold in the wintertime and it was a decent journey to get to Florida, but the beaches were just great, and it was well worth it just to get some sun and heat.

It wasn't just the east coast – we also went to the west coast. I loved driving over there, and one thing I didn't miss was the roundabouts that we get over here in the UK – it's pretty much all straight roads there. If you ever get the chance to go and work over there, then please give it some serious consideration. You won't regret it. Make sure you see as much of the country as you can, and you will meet some great people along the way.

Tell them that Shaun and Carol said hi.

CHAPTER SIXTEEN
Teale On . . .

The best eleven I have played with and why

IN GOAL, I am going for Mark Bosnich. There are several reasons why I chose Bozzie. Simply put, he's the best goalkeeper I have ever played with. Bozzie had an aura around him and he played to the crowd. Who could ever forget his penalty save against Birmingham City in the third round of the League Cup in our successful 1993–1994 campaign, when he basically announced himself to the football world when he came on as substitute for Spinksy at St Andrew's? He just turned round to the partisan home crowd and smiled at them with his arms open wide.

Emi Martinez – eat your heart out!

As a central defender, you need to have complete faith in your teammate who is standing between the sticks, and that was definitely the case with Bozzie. The only chink in the old armour for him was his kicking ability. He couldn't kick for toffee, and the lads were always taking the rise at Bodymoor Heath. He always took it in good faith, though. Bozzie was also as mad as a hatter, and that stood him in good stead, as all the best goalkeepers are! He owned an AK47 gun and would bring it to away games on the coach, pretending to shoot us all with it.

Can you imagine the headlines if it had been loaded?

Can you imagine the headlines now if that happened?

He was a great lad, though, and fun to be around – automatic rifle or not!

At right back, I am going for Earl Barrett. He was not only a great right back, he was one of the fittest players I have ever worked with. He could run all day, that man. If Ron told us we were going for a 50-mile run, every single player except for Earl would moan about it. Earl was a dashing type of player and would always get forward to support the offensive players. He also scored some really important goals for Villa, none more so than the one he scored against Spurs in the League Cup. He was a great person as well, and there were no airs and graces with him – what you saw was what you got with Earl. What you got was greatness.

At left back, I am going for Steve Staunton. Like Earl, he was great at getting up and down the flanks. As I was a left-footed defender, I would find myself covering for him. Stan was a very talented footballer and had come through the Liverpool ranks, and it showed. You always knew when Stan was on the pitch because he was constantly moaning and shouting at you. I guess you can call it keeping me on my toes. It worked very well, especially during the 1992–1993 season. Stan was one of the best crossers of a ball I have ever seen, and we took advantage of that on many occasions. He could also hit a ball as well. The goal he scored against Manchester United in the title clash of 1993 was a brilliant example.

In the centre of defence, I am going to pick myself alongside Paul McGrath. That is not to be conceited or arrogant, but I honestly believe that the relationship I had with Macca, especially during that first Premier League season, was better than most. Only Manchester United (with Pallister and Bruce) and Arsenal (with Adams and Bould) conceded fewer than us that season. We had a wonderful partnership and each knew where the other was at all times, so we could cover for each other. We also got on away from football, and I think this helped our on-field partnership. He would say that I was the legs in the relationship and he was the brains. We always had a good laugh about that. Saying that I had the legs makes it sound like I was happy to run around the pitch, but that was pretty far from the truth. Everyone knows I couldn't run for toffee, and at times I had the brains to get him out of some sticky pickles. We just worked so well together, and I will always cherish my time with him.

In the centre of midfield, I am going for Kevin Richardson. I first got to know Rico when we were both at Everton, and we hit it off from the start. Rico was a complete leader of the team, and it came as no surprise when he was given the captaincy at

Villa. Our wives were very close at the Villa as well, so we often went out as couples. Unfortunately, Francine Richardson passed away a few years back. It devastated Carol and me at the time and still does to this day.

Playing on the left-hand side of midfield would be Andy Townsend. He was probably the most enthusiastic footballer I have ever worked with; his work rate was just brilliant. Andy had the perfect engine to get backwards and forwards, and he scored some brilliant goals for us. Ron brought him to the club in the summer of 1993, and he was just what we needed at the time. He could also command in more central positions when called upon. Andy had the darkest sense of humour I have ever known a footballer to have.

On the right side would be Tony Daley. Dales was a natural winger and had pace in abundance. You knew that once he had the ball at his feet, just about anything could happen. He just never gave up. Cast your mind back to the League Cup semi-final against Tranmere. It was the 88th minute, and he hit a pinpoint cross that Dalian Atkinson scored from. I don't know anybody who has a bad word to say about Dales. He's just an absolutely lovely bloke.

Playing in the number 10 role would be Gordon Cowans. Sid played for Villa on three separate occasions in the 1970s, 1980s and 1990s, and when I speak to players who played with him in those eras, they all tell me that he was one of the best players they have worked with. Just watching Sid in training was a pure joy, let alone seeing him play. He could play a ball with either his right or his left foot and he would find that killer pass. He was a delightful player who would be easily worth around £100 million in this day and age.

My two up front (note that my formation is 4-4-2) would be Dalian Atkinson and Dwight Yorke. When either of those players had the ball and was attacking the opposition, it was genuinely a pleasure to watch them. They were exciting and by no means just six-yard strikers. They were both very capable of picking the ball up deep and moving forward with it as they turned the opposition inside and out, either creating chances themselves or laying it off to colleagues after they'd pulled players out of position. And they could both score goals too.

So my team is a 4-4-2 formation:

Goalkeeper: Bosnich.
Defence: Barrett, McGrath, Teale, Staunton.
Midfield: Daley, Richardson, Cowans, Townsend.
Attack: Atkinson, Yorke.

I could have picked many other players, not just from Aston Villa, but the above are the best players that I played with in my career. They just happen to have all played with me at Villa.

There is a side note to tell you about regarding two of those players. A story that made the front pages of the tabloids also featured some of the rooms from our old house in Sutton Coldfield.

When I signed for Tranmere Rovers, we sold our house to Dwight Yorke. It made sense all round, as Dwight had started to become a regular in the team under Brian Little. Yorkie was obviously fond of showing his house off to other people, and in particular after a night out with Mark Bosnich. So much so that a tape was made with them in our old bedroom with a few members of the opposite sex that they had met up with. I've never seen the contents of the tape, but I am assured that it would not pass the 9 p.m. watershed! Carol and I hadn't seen the tabloids when the story first broke, but we did receive plenty of calls from friends who had recognised certain parts of the house and wondered if we had made the tapes! We very quickly corrected our friends on this matter!

The best game I have played in and why

I loved winning the 1994 League Cup, but for me I would have to say that the semi-final just about trumped the final. I have gone into detail about that match at the start of this book, but it just had everything – the atmosphere, the fact that we had come from behind, and the fact that I was the one who scored the goal that restored parity. Then I converted my spot kick in the shootout. That makes it the greatest game for me.

The worst game I have played in and why

This is an easy one. It was the last home game of the 1992–1993 season when Villa were hosting Oldham Athletic. Even though it was still mathematically possible that we could overthrow Manchester United to win the title, the defeat at Blackburn Rovers the game before had really taken it out of us. We just didn't turn up, and Oldham won the game 1-0 to confirm United as league champions, even though they didn't actually play until the following day. Steve Bruce had a party at his house and Alex Ferguson was on the golf course as the final whistle blew at Villa Park. I have never wanted to get away from the ground as quickly as I did that day.

The best manager I have played for and why

This is an easy one for me – it's Stuart Morgan, the man who took me from Northwich Victoria to Weymouth, which eventually got me the move into the professional leagues. Stuart simply believed in me and knew that all the previous rejections had made me more determined. He invested his time in me. I will always be grateful to Stuart for that. Notable mentions have to go to Cliff Roberts at Northwich Victoria for moving me into a central defensive role, and Harry Redknapp and Ron Atkinson as well. Harry and Ron developed me even further when I became a pro. I may not have approved of some of their methods, but I have to put it on record that they were positive influences on me.

The worst manager I have played for and why

John Aldridge at Tranmere Rovers. His man-management skills were zero when he knew that he would have to get me off the books to fund new acquisitions. All he had to do was speak to me and I would have understood (probably!), but his silence was deafening. The way he just ignored me and cast me out was totally unnecessary and unforgiveable.

Then we have Billy Davies at Motherwell. His backtracking

and lies came to define my time with him. One thing that I did take from him was that it's important to be honest with players and respect that they are not just a commodity. I used that when I became a manager in my own right. Thanks, Billy! I basically did the complete opposite of what you had done.

The best team I have played for and why

Of course I am going to mention Aston Villa, but the same can be said for Tranmere and Bournemouth to a lesser extent. If I search deeper, then I would have to say that it's Northwich Victoria. That team spirit that we developed towards the end of the season when it looked like relegation was a certainty was just amazing, and it eventually took us to safety. I will never forget that.

The worst team I have played for and why

This was the time I turned out for Wigan Athletic after I'd sent letters to clubs asking for trials. I played for them once in a Northern Cup game at Springfield Park. The opposition escapes me, but what didn't escape me was how bad the facilities were at Springfield Park, especially the pitch. I didn't like the way the club was being run. It's obviously different now, but it wasn't good for me at that time.

What advice would you give your younger self and players today and why?

Any player must be prepared for some form of rejection, and you'll need to have a plan for how to address it, even if it's just to keep going and have that self-belief. I had a lot of this. If players today do not have this, then they are in trouble from the start. It can't be coached, but it can be voiced through constant support. The player needs to have fire in their stomach to get through. If they have that, then the next thing to do is listen to their coaches and apply themselves correctly. From there (adding a pinch of luck where applicable), anything is possible.

What do you like to do outside of the game?

I have been very lucky in that I've always had the support and love of my wife, Carol, and my family when I've had to make decisions regarding my career. Some of these decisions have had to be made much more quickly than others. I love the game so very much, but it's my family that has enabled this. Therefore there is nothing better than spending time with Carol, the kids and my grandchildren. I know it's a cliché, but they really are my world. So if it's watching a film, listening to music, being on holiday, as long as it's with them, the world is alright with me.

CHAPTER SEVENTEEN
On Teale . . .

Stuart Morgan
Former Weymouth manager and AFC Bournemouth chief scout

ONE OF THE highlights for me as a manager was bringing through non-league players and turning them into top-flight players. The first time this happened was in 1980 during my first stint as manager of Weymouth FC. The player in question was Graham Roberts. He was an excellent defender for me, who had all the right attributes to go far, and I sold him that year to Tottenham Hotspur.

Graham didn't look back and had a glittering career with Spurs, Rangers, Chelsea and West Bromwich Albion, to name but a few clubs, and he also went on to represent England on a few occasions. I was so proud of what he had achieved, and I honestly didn't think I would find another like him.

However, it was during my second stint as manager of Weymouth that I did indeed find another Graham Roberts. I had been told to go and watch a lad at Northwich Victoria called Shaun Teale. I didn't know that much about him, but what I did know was that he had been around the non-league scene in the northwest. It was a long journey, but when I took my place in the stands, I knew that it had been a very worthwhile one. I watched this young lad with his wavy hair move around the pitch, bossing the central defence. He was vocal and I liked his attitude.

When I got back to Weymouth, I immediately set the ball rolling to sign him, and it was a decision that I did not regret. Weymouth at the time were a very strong club that had the ambition to become a league club, so it was a step up for him, but it never showed. I like players who wear their heart on their sleeve, are positionally aware of where they should be on the pitch, are not afraid to bark orders, take instructions on board and are generally a positive influence on the dressing room. Shaun was all of these and more. I could simply trust him to do a job for me.

It was great when we found ourselves in the professional leagues with Bournemouth. The step up to that level of football was something that Shaun just took in his stride. It was as if he had been playing there all his career. I was so pleased to see him picking up so many Man of the Match awards and winning Player of the Season for consecutive seasons with us. It was only a matter of time before the bigger clubs came looking at him, and the lucky team that got him was Aston Villa.

My son was very close to his son, Nathan, and even became a Villa fan on the back of Shaun's move there. When I look back at my career and think of Shaun, I always smile to myself. Not only was he a great footballer, but he shone as a top person as well. He will always be one of the best players that I signed and easily in my all-time top 11 players that I managed.

I'm honoured that he asked me to contribute to the book and was very pleased when Rob Carless rang me to wax lyrical about Shaun.

That half hour on the phone went very quickly indeed.

Steve Walsh

Former Leicester City captain and part of the coaching staff with Shaun in the USA

When I think about Tealey as a player, he reminds me very much of myself. He was very similar to me in the style of football that we played – we were very tough, no-nonsense centre backs, although in fairness to Tealey, I got sent off much more than he did. I'm still the joint British record holder for that.

Whilst all the above is true, I really liked the way he played, and some of his football was a joy to watch. We have more in common than just the position that we played in as well. We were both born in 1964 and we come from the northwest of England too. Shaun was a posh boy, though, as he was born in

Southport, while I was the poor lad from nearby Preston! We would get to go to Southport on our holidays, and I thought it was just a marvellous place right near the seaside. Tealey got to experience this every day growing up, the lucky bugger!

I think we played around the same number of matches in our respective careers, the main difference being that I was really a one-club type of player, and that club was Leicester City. I do admire the fact that Shaun played for a few clubs before he hit the big time with Villa. I think this kept him grounded and formed a big part of his personality, which was a humble one and a bloke who you could take to and trust.

We locked horns on several occasions in the 1990s, and going up for (or defending) a corner or other set pieces was interesting, to say the least. We hustled and we bustled and we gave no quarter, but it was always firm and fair. He sometimes got the better of me and vice versa. However, the biggest rivalry and the one that hurt the most was when he was player/manager of Burscough. I was at Tamworth on the playing staff, and we met in the FA Trophy final held at Villa Park in 2003. I remember walking around the pitch and doing a pre-match interview with Shaun. We had done the same things in the few days leading up to the final. Tealey was just a fantastic fella and we really hit it off. Tamworth were flying high. We had already won our league and were expected to win the double, although we were never arrogant about it. We simply lost to the better team on the day, and that's football for you. I was gutted to lose the match, as were my teammates, but if we had to lose that day, then I'm glad it was to Shaun. I'm glad it was his team that took the cup home instead.

The next time our paths crossed was in the United States when we did some coaching together. I didn't stay as long as Shaun did, but I had a great time sharing the apartment with him and Carol. They took the time to look after me after the coaching sessions, making sure I was fed and watered. They really are a wonderful couple, and I will always look back on my time coaching in the US with a great deal of fondness and some really happy memories. It's great to see him finally write this book.

Well done, Tealey. You deserve it, pal!

Tony Daley
Former Aston Villa teammate

A footballer's journey can take many roads. There are players like me who came through the youth ranks and hit the big time quicker than those who came via the non-league route. Tealey was one of those players whose journey was full of twists and turns, but I honestly think it made him appreciate what he had at Villa even more. He reminds me of Ian Wright in that respect. A completely different type of player to Tealey, of course, but you can tell that Wrighty enjoyed every minute of his time in professional football. Shaun was the same, making up for lost time and all those rejections he'd had along the way.

When he first joined the Villa, there was no way you could tell his journey, and you would have thought he had been playing top-flight football all his life. He basically took to it like a duck to water. Tealey was an aggressive player, even in training, but he was always fair as well. He never looked like a central defender to me. I always thought he looked more like a midfielder. But the thing was that as soon as he stepped onto the pitch, you knew exactly why he was in the position that Big Ron had signed him for. He fitted in very well with Derek Mountfield and Paul McGrath at the heart of our defence, and later with Ugo as his Villa career progressed.

Tealey was very vocal on the pitch and he would be on your back if silly mistakes were made, but what I loved about playing with him was that he was quick to give out the praise when required as well. He had the biggest calves I have ever seen, and boy, could he play on that left foot of his. I clearly remember some great balls played to me from him that weren't simply just a hoof and hope for the best, and I turned round and clapped him a few times when we played together.

He was also a great influence in the dressing room as well as at Bodymoor Heath in our many training sessions and also away from the game. Tealey was fun to be around and also very serious about his footballing duties. We simply just got on, and he was a pleasure to play and work with. He was a great lad to know as well.

I also liked the fact that he was a big family man. You would always see Carol and the boys in and around the club, and the Teales always had time to speak to you. I still see Shaun at Villa Park today. I was born just a stone's throw from the ground and he came from Southport, which is miles away, but he is as much of a fan of the Villa as I am, and that's great. His knowledge of the club is something else as well. I always look forward to seeing him and catching up and having a good laugh together.

You know where you stand with people like Tealey.

John Gidman

Former Everton, Manchester United and Aston Villa right back

I first became aware of Shaun Teale at Everton in the late 1970s and early 1980s. He was an apprentice and I was a first-team player. You know the young lads who will make it in the game and the ones that won't. It's not just the football ability that they possess but also their attitude. Tealey stuck out for me because he had good skills and was willing to learn from the professionals who had come before him, so I knew he was going to make it. Another player that I knew would also make it was Mark Ward, who was also part of the youth set-up.

Everton had some good youngsters coming through and they had formed a good team. Everyone was raving about the players coming through at Liverpool, but some of ours were just as good. I then went on to play for Manchester United under Ron Atkinson. The next time I heard about Shaun was when he signed for the Villa in the early part of the 1990s with Big Ron at the helm. It's funny how football turns out. Tealey and I were both at the same club at the same time but at different parts of our career paths; he would go on to play for my former club Aston Villa under my former gaffer at Manchester United.

I was so pleased to see Shaun sign for the Villa. I still have strong ties to the club. He was a player that gave his all, and he formed great partnerships with Paul McGrath and others. Shaun was the type of player that I would have liked to have played with in the defensive department. I would have been on the right, and he would have been on the left-hand side supporting the left backs. You knew he was a player that you could trust to do the job and basically help out when needed. He should have played for England in my opinion.

In a lot of ways, his career reminds me of mine, especially in the early years. I got a rejection letter from Bill Shankly when I was at Liverpool and would have been roughly the same age as Shaun was when he was at Everton with me. The rejection spurred me on. I became determined to make it as a full-time professional footballer, which I did at Aston Villa in the early 1970s. I know that Shaun has received similar types of letters in the past and they seemed to spur him on. He ultimately found it in him to succeed and achieve his goals. He deserves a lot of credit for that, and I am pleased to see that he has worked with Rob Carless (who I have worked with in the past myself) in bringing out this book.

I very much look forward to reading it.

Nice one, Tealey!

Ray Stafford
Burscough, Northwich Victoria and Chorley assistant manager

I knew that Shaun had played for Southport at the beginning of his career, but it was when he rejoined us at the end of his career that I really got to know him, and we hit it off straight away. I was training the second team at the time, and after a match, he came over to me and told me that I should be taking the first team, not the second string. He didn't have to do that, as he wasn't actually playing, but he took the time to come and see me. I never forgot that, and from then on, our relationship really flourished.

Shaun was coming to the end of his playing days and was ready to advance his career by going into management. If I recall correctly, his last game playing for Southport was at home to Woking. I saw him in the corridor after the match and wished him luck for whatever he decided to do in football. I knew he had played his last game for Southport and I was genuinely sorry to see him go. It was at this point that he told me that Burscough were interested in him taking over as manager for the 2002–2003 season. He asked me if I would consider coming with him as his assistant. I couldn't believe it. One minute I am saying goodbye to him and wishing him luck, and the next, I am being offered a job as his assistant! It didn't take too long for me to say yes.

We got together soon afterwards to agree a strategy regarding pre-season activities and preparation for the next season. He was very professional, and if I hadn't known it was his first managerial role, I would have sworn he had been doing it for years. We brought in some younger players and some lads that had played non-league football and the lower divisions in the Football League. The FA Trophy journey was incredible. We started off the cup campaign with a little bit of luck on our side, but we were soon motoring and upsetting the odds as we reached the final, with Shaun still playing as well as managing the team.

He was great with the players and he was great with me as well. When he was on the pitch and I was running the team from the benches, he never once questioned my decisions or tried to overturn a decision I made and pull rank, even if I thought it right to bring him off. That was the mark of the man and to me proved that it was all about what was right for the team and not all about Shaun Teale.

It was so apt that the final against Tamworth was played at Villa Park in May 2003. That was really where the football world took notice of him. It had been years since he had left Villa, but he still had the right connections and was obviously still very much liked at the club. He arranged for us to use the facilities at Bodymoor Heath, where the Villa trained, and the club even washed and ironed our kit for the final. It made us feel like a Premier League club.

We had gone down to Birmingham with the team on the Thursday night, even though the Burscough board had wanted us to travel down on the Sunday, which was the actual day of the final. Shaun was having none of it and insisted they stick to his plan. Luckily, he won out, and I firmly believe that the players really benefited from having the Premier League experience. I believe it was a major factor in us winning the trophy.

The highlight for me (apart from managing the team while Shaun played in the final) was getting to meet Doug Ellis, Villa's chairman, and spending time with him in his office with Shaun.

It was basically a catch-up between a chairman and an ex-player. For me, though, I have to admit that I was a little starstruck. I met a few big and important people in the game because of my association with Shaun. As always, he took it in his stride, but I was always registering that I was standing with someone like Brian Clough while being in awe of the great man. Shaun never saw anyone like that at all, because he treated everyone the same. He would spend as much time working with players who had faced some form of rejection, like he had done in the past, as he did with the big hitters. I loved that about him.

I followed him to Northwich Victoria and Chorley as his assistant when he took the managerial reins at both clubs. I was absolutely gutted when he announced that he was retiring from the game. I think he had fallen out of love with it by the time he took over the running of the pub. It was football's loss and the pub trade's gain, if you ask me!

I still keep in touch with him, and we are the best of mates. I love his family too. To this day, I ask him if he is going to give football management another shot and remind him that he still has it in him. I've told him that I will go with him again if he ever changes his mind. I would jump at the chance to light that flame again with Tealey!

Derek McGregor

Local football reporter at Bournemouth and Motherwell

Shaun was tough as teak with his boots on, as hard a defender as I've seen in my near 40 years covering football.

But Shaun's always been just as unflinching with his opinions.

Mercifully, I never had to suffer a bone-shuddering tackle from him.

However, back in my fledgling days as a reporter – I was 22 when I first started getting to know Shaun while I was AFC Bournemouth correspondent for the local *Evening Echo* newspaper – I did endure the odd, I'll put it politely, disapproving verdict from him over a match analysis. Imagine also how he felt whenever I felt the need to give him 5 out of 10 for a performance. (Not often, though!)

That sparked the verbal equivalent of a studs-up challenge

to the knee. "Are you f****** sure, McGregor?" he'd holler at me first chance he got.

Back in those days of 1990 and 1991, just before his life-changing big-time move to Aston Villa, Shaun was one of a good number of formidable senior pros at the Cherries, and dealing with them all was a priceless experience for a relatively raw reporter. It set me up for the rest of my career.

Shaun was brilliant with me, like everyone else at the club, to be fair. He's a proper man's man.

On the park he gave it out, took it back. His 'take no prisoners' style helped him as a centre half to intimidate strikers. I can't imagine he ever got the proverbial ripped out of him for his porn-star moustache.

Shaun wasn't just a hard man, he was a top defender with a tremendous left foot while he was outstanding, too, in the air. Should've got an England cap.

He moved to the Midlands and we kept in touch, but then a few years passed without contact until 1998. With me back working in Scotland, he stunningly joined Motherwell. By then I was a national football writer, and I was thrilled we could pick up from where we'd left off.

Shaun's always been a journalist's dream in the category of great talker. Selfishly, I knew I would benefit again from our excellent relationship – and oh, how I did.

Shaun memorably ended his Fir Park spell with a sensational public blast at the then Motherwell owner, John Boyle, over a contract wrangle, accusing him of 'leading me up the garden path'.

It was a dynamite exclusive.

After 32 years, I'm proud Shaun's become as much a valued friend as a great contact.

Gary Fox
Aston Villa supporter – travelled home and away when Shaun played for the club

In the early 1990s, if Shaun Teale's arrival at Villa Park was greeted with a 'Shaun who?' by 99% of the Holte Enders awaiting big name signings, it didn't take us long to work out exactly what this new defender of ours was all about!

The year was 1991 and football was on the brink of changing forever. Football and Gazza had won the hearts of the nation at the 1990 World Cup and also through the vision, imagination and wallets of the advertisers and salespeople in the City of London.

A new Premier League was born. Football was to appeal to all and was the new story in town!

As those advertisers from Saatchi & Saatchi looked for clean-cut, good-looking goal scorers to attract those new customers, young girls and high-flyers from the West End wine bars, Aston Villa had gone out and bought themselves a throwback from another era – a steady, solid centre half who looked like he'd be more comfortable next to us on a Friday night in the local pub before the latest bar room brawl was about to break out!

A real spit-and-sawdust hero to boot. He was Our Shaun.

In fact, in that throwback kit from the 1992–1993 season, he looked like an original from the Victorian era with the lace through the shirt and the baggy shorts. There stood Shaun – he of the massive thighs and unfussy hair. And that moustache!

I believe his arrival in the starting line-up was a surprise on that iconic opening day of the never-to-be-forgotten win at Sheffield Wednesday. It certainly raised a few eyebrows, but it didn't take him long to cement his place in the claret and blue. In fact, he was a mainstay in a wonderful attacking, good footballing side in a successful trophy-winning era.

Shaun and Paul McGrath formed one of the greatest partnerships of my time supporting the Villans. There's been few better from my place watching them from the famous Holte End.

These pair were majestic – silk and steel, and make no mistake, both could be either at any given moment.

For every Paul McGrath interception, there was a Teale 'coming through the pack to head away' moment. For every one of God's back-flicks, there'd be a big crunching Shaun Teale tackle. Make no mistake, though, Shaun wasn't a dirty player. Quite the opposite, in fact. He was as honest as the day was long. As honest as he'd never shirk a tackle. As honest as he never gave less than 100% in every game. As honest as he was never less than an 8 out of 10 for effort in every performance.

There were many great days to remember during the Teale years. Those were great times; he was an exceptional player in a phenomenal team, but it would be remiss of me to mention Shaun without mentioning that never-to-be-forgotten Sunday afternoon of 27 February 1994.

Well, in true enigmatic Villa style, after drawing the minnows in the semi-final, Villa had done their utmost at Prenton Park to throw away their chances of Wembley glory – a 3-1 defeat and outplayed on the night. An unexplainably poor performance was given a positive spin with a 90th-minute Dalian Atkinson strike.

That night we left Tranmere believing that the dream was over – or did we?

In the second leg, Our Shaun had decided on that given Sunday that he would not walk off that pitch without giving every bit of his effort, heart, nerve, sinew and blood to reversing our fortunes. The game, spoken of elsewhere, ebbed and flowed to and fro. A rare Shaun goal seemed to have put Villa in the box seat, but they seemed to do their best to break our hearts. It was to be anything other than straightforward. The greatest rollercoaster game fans had ever seen saw Villa snatch glory from the hands of defeat in a penalty shootout, and Shaun's performance that day shone like a beacon.

The cup was brought back to Birmingham as the champions of England, Manchester United, were defeated on the hallowed Wembley turf.

In a strange sort of way, it seemed as quietly as Shaun entered Villa Park, in the August of 1995, he departed the scene of his greatest success in high-level football.

Sad times. But he'll never be forgotten by Villans of that beautiful era.

Our cult hero, yeah, even if others were quicker and some scored more, but he was that no-nonsense guy you identified with, loved by the claret and blue faithful.

It's hard to look back at that era of heady days and Shaun Teale without a smile. He was a man who never gave less than everything he had for us. "A working-class hero is something to be . . ." is a famous line from a John Lennon song. And that's what you are to me, Shaun.

Statistics And Honours

Data source: English National Football Archive and Wikipedia.

	Appearances	Goals
Southport 1983—1988	112	6
Weymouth 1988—1989	100	4
AFC Bournemouth 1989—1991	116	5
Aston Villa 1991—1995	181	5
Tranmere Rovers 1995—1998	62	0
Preston North End (loan) 1997	5	0
Happy Valley (loan) 1997—1998	25	3
Motherwell 1998—2000	52	4
Carlisle United 2000	20	0
Southport 2000—2002	68	5
Burscough 2002—2003	12	0
Northwich Victoria 2003—2004	6	1
Total	**759**	**33**

Teams managed
2002–2003: Burscough
2003–2004: Northwich Victoria
2005–2006: Chorley

Honours

League Cup - Aston Villa	Winners	1994
FA Trophy - Burscough	Winners	2003

ACKNOWLEDGEMENTS

FOR A FEW years now, I have been thinking about writing my football memoirs. I guess the reason it never happened previously was time, and maybe I didn't think it would be of interest to people. With the outbreak of COVID in 2020, it gave me some time to reflect on the book, and I was glad to speak to Simon Goodyear about the project – and now here we are.

There are a number of people to thank, and perhaps the story would have little or no credence without them.

Top of the list, of course, is my wife, Carol. I knew I wanted to be with this woman the day I first clapped eyes on her, and we have never looked back. Her support for my career has never ever wavered, and we've had some laughs and tears along the way. I love the woman so much, and I owe her everything. She gave me two wonderful boys who in turn have provided me with wonderful grandchildren. I have to thank my mum and dad and the Teale family in general for their love and support when I was growing up. It has been invaluable.

In terms of people in the game, especially during those early years, I need to mention Tony Rimmer, who was my very first manager in football. He was a guiding light to me. Unfortunately, Tony passed away in the latter part of 2022. Thanks so much, Tony, and RIP.

Sam Benbow and his family also deserve major credit. I will always love the minibus that he bought that carried us all around the area.

Graham Smith, reserve and youth team coach at Everton, was a major influence on me when I was at Goodison Park, as was Bob Murphy at Southport. Both guys were strict disciplinarians, but they did it for all the right reasons. Thanks to Cliff Roberts at Northwich Victoria, who (a) made me a central defender, and (b) sold me to Weymouth, which opened major doors for me. Which leads me nicely on to Stuart Morgan. Meeting and playing for Stuart was *the* defining moment in my career. His belief in me was nothing short of excellent and allowed me to move to professional football. He was probably the most important person in my career outside of my family. A truly wonderful person.

From Stuart, I went to Harry Redknapp and then Ron Atkinson as I progressed to top-flight football. How can I not thank them for this? Brian Little deserves major acknowledgement for a number of reasons. Firstly, penning the foreword for me and secondly, being totally honest about his decision to sell me, which resulted in me and my family obtaining financial security.

I played with some great players, and some of them turned out to be great people as well. I could name so many – they know who they are, but I feel that this is the right time to mention Paul McGrath. The four years that I spent with him as my partner in football crime were the best I could ever have imagined. A truly beautiful soul. Cheers, Macca.

I would like to thank the chairmen as well. Doug Ellis (RIP) deserves a mention, as does Frank Parr at Burscough. OK, in terms of Frank it turned sour, but I will always be grateful to him for giving me my first chance in football management.

The fans of the clubs I played for deserve a mention as well. They were always great with me and to Carol and the boys. I will always have a beer with them. They make football what it is.

A special thanks to Simon Goodyear for believing in the book and for introducing me to Barrie Pierpoint, Mathew Mann and the team at Morgan Lawrence, who published it. Thanks to Lee Clark for the cover, Peter Andrews and Catherine Dunn for editing and proofreading, Holly Mann for typesetting, and Peter Taylor and Harry Worgan for the marketing and social media campaigns. Thanks for believing in me.

Also, massive gratitude to the following people and organisations for sponsoring my book. I am truly grateful for this. Steve Jones – Crown Highways, Duncan Mathieson – Realis Estates, Mark Thomas – 1st Safety, Karl O'Neill – Tomkinson Teal.

I'd also like to thank Luke Roper – Luke1977, who has

sponsored my book tour and the marketing campaign to promote my events.

A big thanks to Rob Carless, who helped me write this book. Apparently, his job was as a 'ghost writer'. I didn't even know they existed! I am aware of them now, but I can call him a friend these days. I thoroughly enjoyed our calls, Zoom meetings, and him coming up to Southport for a couple of days to spend time with me and the family. Cheers, Rob – a top bloke.

And finally, many thanks to you for taking the time to read this book. I hope you enjoyed it and it gave you a good insight into what it's like to play football at various levels. Never give up on your dreams, despite those who tell you it won't happen.

Maybe it's a life lesson as well as a football one.

Cheers.

Shaun Teale

Duncan Mathieson

Realis Estates

AS AN ABERDONIAN, you may wonder where my love for Aston Villa came from. Well, as a six-year-old in 1975 when Andy Gray joined Aston Villa, my brother said, "That is the English team we will support" – alongside Aberdeen, of course. My passion for the club grew and grew from there through TV, radio and reading about the club.

When Big Ron signed Shaun, I followed his career closely, and his formidable partnership with Paul McGrath was superb.

My highlight of his Villa career was when we beat Man United in the Coca-Cola Cup final 3-1 – what a great day. It was a superb team performance.

I have been fortunate, since 2007, to have season tickets at Villa Park and have the chance to catch up with Villa legends on a regular basis. Shaun's career at Villa may have been short, but he is still very active with the club and in my eyes is a true Aston Villa legend.

Shaun, I wish you all the very best with the book, and I am proud that I personally can be involved in bringing it to print along with my company Realis Estates.

Realis Estates are property developers/managers and specialise in developing commercial property throughout the UK.

www.realisestates.co.uk

Realis Estates Limited

Steve Jones

Crown Highways, Chasetown FC and lifelong Villan.

AS VILLA FANS, we are fortunate to have a proud, successful and illustrious history, ensuring that each and every one of us is proud to support this great club.

Like all football supporters, we are constantly asked to recall our most memorable game, favourite player and best goal – an impossible task.

However, one of my greatest Villa Park memories was of Big Ron's old guard in the semi-final of the Coca-Cola Cup in the 1994–1995 season. I can still see Shaun Teale's diving header that put us level and his big moustache-covered smile beaming even before the ball hit the back of the net. Arms spread wide, Villa Park jumping, a claret and blue sea of unbridled joy and madness. That night was indeed one of those super-special occasions.

We've been blessed over the years with some incredible defenders – McGrath, Ugo, Southgate, Mellberg, Evans, McNaught, and I'm delighted to say Shaun Teale belongs in that illustrious group. His pairing with Paul McGrath was special, and of course the stories aren't bad either.

In my 48 years of being a fan, I've had season tickets in every part of the ground, each location special for different reasons. I'm fortunate now, in my mid-50s, that I am able to sit amongst corporate friends and chat to former players about seasons gone by and, of course, the modern day game.

Shaun Teale is certainly one of those former heroes who epitomises the down-to-earth nature of the game gone by. Shaun and his wife, Carol, are wonderful people, and I'm delighted that I could play a tiny part in making this book achievable.

Well done and very best wishes, Shaun – you will always be a Villa legend.

UTV.

Mark Thomas

1st Safety

SHAUN WAS A real hero of mine because me and a few friends started going to all the home and away games in the early 1990s, and the partnership between Shaun, Ugo and Paul McGrath was unbelievable.

Shaun was hard, brave and had a never-say-die attitude. People say you should never meet your heroes, but in Shaun's case this could not be further from the truth. He is a true gentleman and legend.

Good luck with the book.

UTV.

Karl O'Neill

Tomkinson Teal

I RECALL WHEN Aston Villa (a club I have followed for over 50 years) signed Shaun Teale in 1991. I must admit he was a player I knew nothing of.

Very quickly, however, it became very apparent that he was a traditional, no-nonsense centre half who took no prisoners, and he soon formed an incredible defensive partnership with one Paul McGrath. I spent many a day both home and away during the years Shaun served the club and I can't recall any game where he never put himself on the line to serve the mighty Villa.

Some highlights spring to mind – the League Cup semi-final against Tranmere, where he lashed his penalty in, and then beating Manchester United in the final at Wembley. The altercation with a Grimsby player on a cold January day away in the FA Cup, where I think he lost his shirt, just proved how tough he was.

I have had the pleasure of meeting Shaun a few times when he attends the hospitality areas at Aston Villa, and I can honestly say I always enjoy his pre- and post-match comments.

When I was asked to be part of the sponsorship team for his book, it was a no-brainer. I was more than happy to help.

Karl O'Neill is a partner in Tomkinson Teal, Chartered Accountants, based in Lichfield, Staffordshire.

Luke Roper

LUKE1977

Shaun was part of my all-time favourite Villa centre back pairing, a colossus alongside Paul McGrath. Both were honest, hard as nails and gentlemen. He thrived in an era when the game was played with G-force over G-wagons and when social skills, not social media, were the order of the day.

Almost 30 years on, the world and the game have changed so much. Memories of my first Wembley visit in March 1994 live strong. I was a fresh-faced 16-year-old lad with a wispy tache – Shaun had the real thing!

A minibus left from Walsall Wood; I tagged on, joining my brother Mark and his friends. Mark first took me to Villa Park as a seven-year-old, and I have him to thank for my love of the club. My mom knitted me a claret and blue jumper, so retro looking (even at the time), that's now in a frame. We dipped in and out of the pubs around the ground, taking in the pre-game atmosphere. Shaun's defensive header was the last touch of the game. The rest is history, and beating Manchester United at Wembley will live with me forever.

I'm proud to know Shaun and it's an honour to be involved with his book. He will always be a Villa legend.

A NOTE FROM THE AUTHOR
Rob Carless

WHEN I WAS approached by my agent, Simon Goodyear, to work with Shaun Teale on his autobiography, I jumped at the chance to do so. I had seen Shaun play many times during his spell at Aston Villa and in recent years have been privy to his contributions on social media. On both platforms I found that Shaun would wear his heart on his sleeve, and for that reason, I knew he would be a great subject.

I spent a great deal of time with Shaun face to face, over the phone and on Zoom calls, and he gave me everything I needed to write this book. A ghost writer's job is to get to the heart of the subject and then turn it into prose. In a nutshell, I found out pretty early in the process that he was a footballer and a person with principles.

Shaun firmly believes that footballers should not be made to be commodities and that the game can be very cruel at times to those it throws on the scrapheap. He faced rejection multiple times during his playing career but was always determined to go as far as he could – which was right to the top. Indeed, it struck me just how much this meant to him when he went into management and made sure that he did in fact put his players first. Maybe this was a major reason why he fell out with people in boardrooms at times.

Shaun made it a delight for me to carry out my tasks, and so did Carol. They truly are a wonderful couple, a partnership and also great people in their own right. On one occasion during the interviews, we spent time looking through a box of old press cuttings and photos. It was a fascinating couple of hours, and you could feel the pride and care that had been taken in Shaun's very own box of tricks of a lifetime kicking and heading a football.

I was drawn to an article written by Derek McGregor of the *Bournemouth Echo* where he described Shaun as "A proud Northerner and patter merchant." I could not concur more. McGregor goes on to add that "Teale has a close bond with Cherries supporters," as he did at all the other clubs he played for. He was a player you could trust; he is also a person you can trust as well.

Also, many thanks to Paul, Andrea, Ryan, Aime, Rhys and Hannah for all their support.

MORGAN LAWRENCE
PUBLISHING SERVICES

"MINDING MY OWN FOOTBALL BUSINESS"
The inside story of Leicester City's success in the 90s.
FILBERT STREET LE2
By Barrie Pierpoint
Leicester City's first Chief Executive
with Mathew Mann
Foreword by Steve Walsh

WHAT IF?
AN ALTERNATIVE HISTORY OF LEICESTER CITY
MATHEW MANN
FOREWORD BY
JULIAN JOACHIM

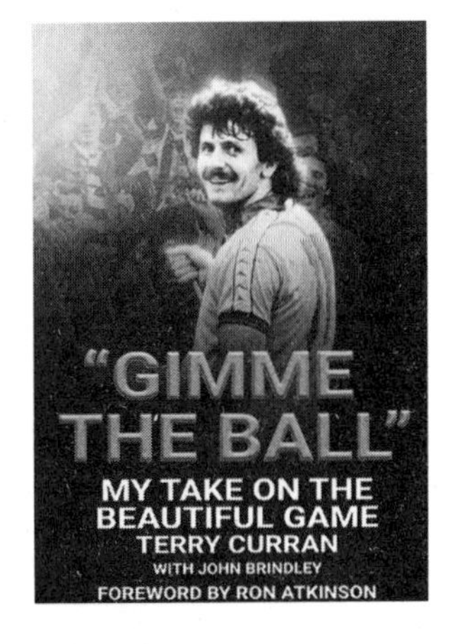
"GIMME THE BALL"
MY TAKE ON THE BEAUTIFUL GAME
TERRY CURRAN
WITH JOHN BRINDLEY
FOREWORD BY RON ATKINSON

JULIAN JOACHIM
My Life In Football
YOU MUST BE JOACHIM

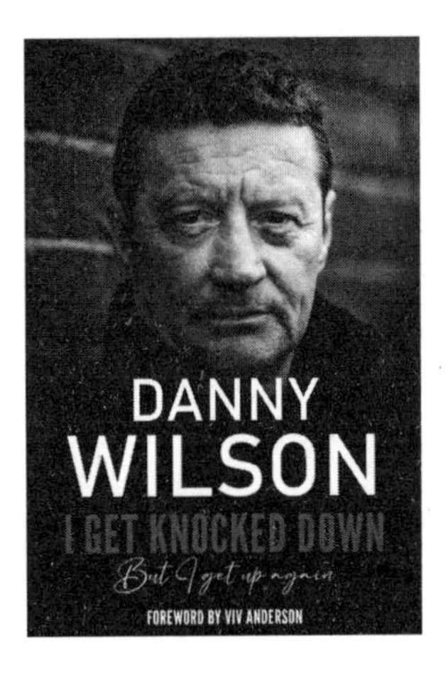
DANNY
WILSON
I GET KNOCKED DOWN
But I get up again
FOREWORD BY VIV ANDERSON

MORGAN LAWRENCE
PUBLISHING SERVICES

The following books are available to purchase from Morgan Lawrence and all major book retailers

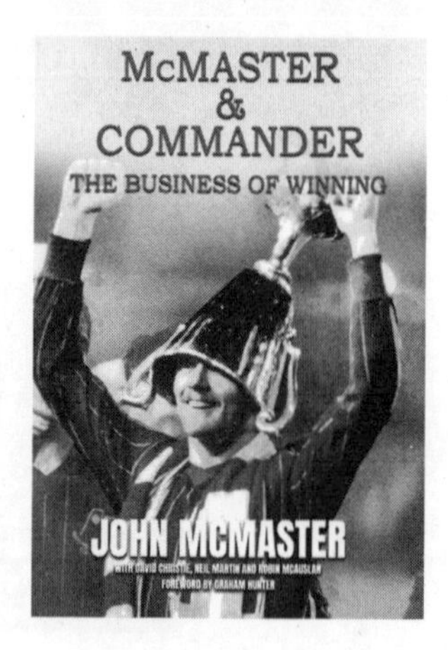

Email: hello@morganlawrence.co.uk
www.morganlawrence.co.uk